TOO YOUNG,
TOO LOUD,
TOO DIFFERENT

TOO
YOUNG

Edited by Maisie Lawrence
& Rishi Dastidar

TOO
LOUD

Poems from Malika's
Poetry Kitchen

TOO
DIFFERENT

corsair *poetry*

CORSAIR POETRY

First published in Great Britain in 2021 by Corsair Poetry

1 3 5 7 9 10 8 6 4 2

A CIP catalogue record for this book is available from the British Library.

ISBN 978-1-4721-5506-1

Typeset in Arno by M Rules
Printed and bound in Great Britain by
Clays Ltd, Elcograf S.p.A.

Papers used by Corsair are from well-managed forests
and other responsible sources.

Corsair
An imprint of
Little, Brown Book Group
Carmelite House,
50 Victoria Embankment
London EC4Y 0DZ

An Hachette UK Company
www.hachette.co.uk

www.littlebrown.co.uk

For Bernardine Evaristo, Kwame Dawes and June Jordan
who shared their recipes –

and Malika and Roger, who cooked them up.

Contents

Foreword

Malika Booker

Together, we aspire together we achieve used to be posted on billboards all across the Guyanese highroads. As a young child I would lip-read this slogan on each sign that my father's car passed, and now seriously believe that those words imprinted the power of the collective onto my soul.

The idea for Malika's Poetry Kitchen sprang from an ongoing creative conversation with my friend and fellow poet Roger Robinson. I recall us sharing a meal in the kitchen of my Brixton flat, talking about poetics, poets we'd recently discovered, and the impact that the Afro-Style School (a writing initiative for Black poets run by the writer development agency Spread the Word, and taught by Forward Prize-winning poet Kwame Dawes) had on our work.

I have a fuzzy recollection of us, over that meal, discussing how writing communities like the Harlem Renaissance, the Negritude Movement and the Caribbean Artist Movement had created some of the best writers of our time. I quoted an African proverb – 'A family that eats together, stays together' – and began to dream of a space where Black writers could gather, eat and develop their craft. Then Roger said, 'What are we waiting for? Let's just do it.' Here, we said, in this house. Friday. Next week. We would call it Malika's Poetry Kitchen.

All that week, in the lead-up to the first workshop, we recruited writers at poetry events, spreading the invitation by word of mouth; to this day this is how Kitchen recruits – every new member joins through personal invitation.

Frankly, Roger and I had no idea what we were doing. We both saw writing as an art that we wanted to master, we were hungry to begin our apprenticeship – yet the literary establishment ridiculed us. They felt that we were only interested in

1

performing, that we were rappers, that our work was not of sufficient quality, and that black bodies like ours had no place at the table. We knew that black and brown bodies, working class voices, women's voices, did not have a space where they could be heard – and so this writing collective was a necessary and political act. We turned to June Jordan's book *Poetry for the People: A Revolutionary Blueprint.* This was our guide, our template, our bible. The ethos of Malika's Poetry Kitchen was formed from four of Jordan's principles, found on the second page of the book:

> **How to** make sure that every single wannabe poet becomes a distinctive voice that people will listen to

> **How to** assure the creation of a community of trust despite serious and sometimes conflictual baseline components of diversity: race, language, sexuality, class, age and gender

> **How to** set up things up so that student poets become teacher poets

> **How to** rescue the 'Canon' from well-deserved disrepute and make it relevant again

Our fifth principle came directly from Kwame Dawes:

> The art and craft of writing is dependent on reading. One cannot develop as a poet if one is not reading.

We wanted to pay forward Kwame's generosity; everyone needed to benefit from the treasures we had gained.

At a later date, we invited Jacob Sam-La Rose to jointly lead Malika's Poetry Kitchen alongside Roger and myself. For over eight years the three of us devoted every Friday night to leading this poetry collective's gatherings. And we succeeded beyond our wildest expectations.

We could never have foreseen the national and international impact the collective would have on the British literary scene. That Peter Kahn would start a branch of Malika's Poetry Kitchen in Chicago. That Peter and Jacob would set up the London Teenage Poetry Slam. That in 2020 Roger Robinson would win the T. S. Eliot Prize, one of the world's most prestigious poetry prizes.

Or that Malika's Poetry Kitchen's commitment and dedication would lead to this twentieth anniversary anthology. I write this a week after our first Zoom poetry workshop, led by Arji Manuelpillai, feeling assured that no matter what happens in the world nothing hampers our meeting on Friday nights. When I also consider the waiting list of poets eager to join the collective, I cannot help but marvel at how far we have come since that initial discussion in my kitchen twenty years ago.

The Secret Knock:
A history of Malika's Poetry Kitchen

Daniel Kramb

ONE

A Friday in August, 2001. A bedroom on Fairmount Road, Brixton. Against the orange wall neat piles of jeans, a long row of trainers. The room is Malika Booker's, but she's not here yet. On the floor near the futon two women are crouched next to one another. Patricia Foster and Janett Plummer. Others have found elsewhere to sit. By the wall a shy American leans, watching. Peter Kahn.

Then, suddenly, a towering figure bounds in, wearing his trademark hat. *Alright. Let's get started.* Roger Robinson.

It's the second session of a collective that have no idea that they are about to begin something that will have a groundbreaking influence on the poetry scene in the UK, affect hundreds of poets in this country and beyond, and help place a new generation of voices into the landscape.

*

In 2001 the popularity of a certain type of poetry is on a high. Every night of the week words are being woven, in cafés and bars, galleries and pubs. The spirit is of experimentation; there is a sense of possibility.

But this 'performance poetry' or 'spoken word' is happening underground. Where it rises to the surface, it comes up against a brutal, seemingly impenetrable barrier. These labels aren't just used to classify, but to keep in place. From *down below*: the experienced, but unrecorded, experimental, electrifying scene.

And then *up there*, bright and elevated, talked and written about: the part of the poetry world that self-consciously calls itself 'page poetry', meant to last, meant to be more prestigious.

A week earlier, Patricia and Janett are on their way to a poetry workshop in Hammersmith. There is no particular reason for them to go through Charing Cross that night, but Janett suggests they do. Walking through the station, they see a tall man approaching. They recognise the hat.

You gotta come. You gotta come! Roger is buzzing with the infectious, insistent energy people know him for. They just had their first meeting (only three people were there). *Why don't you come next week? We'll do it again. Come next Friday!*

Patricia hasn't been sure about her poetry for some time. She feels confused about where it's going next, what she wants it to do. On the train afterwards, she has a strange, overwhelming feeling. *I have to do this.*

Page poetry – in magazines, newspapers, journals, books – is, in 2001, over-whelmingly white. The shortlists of the Forward Prizes for Poetry: white. The shortlist of the T. S. Eliot Prize. Every editor of every journal of note: white. Almost every one of their pages. When the first group of Next Generation Poets is drawn up in 2004, there is no Black or Asian poet on it. A frantic call goes out for ethnic names to be submitted.

On the morning of the collective's second meeting, Peter is standing outside the Centerprise bookshop on Kingsland High Street in Dalston. The young educator has only just arrived in London from Chicago. He knows very little about poetry. In fact, up until recently, he has actively hated it. Hated reading it, hated teaching it. But when a student takes him to a poetry slam, a lightbulb goes on. Now he's in London to learn as much as he can about using poetry in teaching. But he doesn't know anybody. Asking around, someone tells him: *You should speak to Malika Booker.*

Peter pushes the door open and enters the community bookshop where Malika is currently working. She is standing behind the counter. They start talking. Peter tells her he works in a school.

Malika is interested.

So, are you a poet?
Well, I write with my students ...
Okay, so you are a poet.

She tears out a small piece of paper and writes on it. She hands it over. It's an address in Brixton.

When Peter knocks on Malika's door at 7 p.m. that night, punctual as always, someone other than Malika opens the door. He is invited in: *The bedroom is upstairs.* As he heads up, Malika rushes down, ready to go out. *Oh hi, Peter. A* poet she has admired for years, Ruth Forman, is in town. *I need to see her, but you stay here. Can you let people in?* Left alone, Peter sits himself down in the bedroom of someone he has only just met. But it's not long before others ring the doorbell.

*

Malika Booker is born in London, to Guyanese and Grenadian parents. She moves away to spend eleven years of her childhood with her mother, father and two brothers in Guyana. Two important things happen to her: she discovers a love of storytelling, and she lives through a deeply conflicted relationship with her grandmother which, years later, will inform much of her poetry.

She begins writing and performing aged nineteen. A decade later, the theatre follows: one-woman shows, a musical. Her debut stage show, *Absolution*, gets commissioned by the Austrian Cultural Institute and Apples & Snakes; it premieres at the Battersea Arts Centre in 1999. Her first published poem appears in *Bittersweet: Contemporary Black Women's Poetry* the same year.

Halfway through her early career, Malika is studying anthropology at Goldsmiths, University of London. She likes it, but the final year is torturous: all around her, poet friends are performing in London, across the country, abroad. Malika is a little jealous. She wants to be with this crowd. By the time her final exam comes, she's clear with herself. *It's poetry now, or nothing.* Everything she does, from this moment on, is to facilitate her career as a poet. She refuses to claim unemployment benefit, or work in any other field, until it happens. Her flatmates are supportive, let her pay less rent. They understand. Everyone knows how serious she is about this.

Malika meets Roger's sister before she meets Roger. The three become friends. Suddenly, Roger is everywhere. At the soul and calypso concerts Malika loves. At hip hop events. Seeing the Roots, the Fugees. She attends some live arts event at the ICA, and who is there? Roger Robinson. At almost any literary event she goes to. Always scribbling into his small notebook.

Roger is acutely aware that if you are Black, no matter how good you are as a poet, people don't see you. If, every now and again, a door opens to let some

7

people through, it soon shuts again. And if you find yourself on the margins, anywhere outside of it, the *poetry world* can look and feel not just out of reach, but completely impenetrable.

Roger feels – painfully, every day – how every structure is against him, and poets like him. Many give up. But Roger pushes on, keeps saying to others: *We are all going to write! We are all going to continue! This crazy shit won't grind us down.*

Like Malika, Roger is born in London (in Hackney), moves away as a child (aged four, to Trinidad), and returns to the UK (when he's nineteen). In Trinidad, he listens to his mother, a great storyteller, at the dinner table, and grows a love for words, for language.

In the UK, he ends up in Ilford, Essex, and initially lives with his grandmother. It's a culture shock. Eventually, he will pack his bags and settle in Brixton, the neighbourhood he will relentlessly observe, negotiate and turn into art for decades to come. There's a lot of back and forth, a life between the UK and Trinidad, before, years down the line, Roger decides: *I'm here. I'm Black British.*

In London he starts performing with dub bands, becomes the lead vocalist for the crossover project King Midas Sound, records solo albums. The man is music; but the man is poetry first.

By now, Malika has found a job. Apples & Snakes – founded in the early eighties by a group of poets in a room above a pub and speedily growing into the country's leading spoken-word poetry organisation – have hired her as their education co-ordinator. Shortly after she joins, they bring in Roger as their programmer: the two friends are now also colleagues.

In a derelict building in Deptford, Malika is brainstorming ideas for new shows, plotting, initiating. She watches, listens, absorbs. She makes connections. Her kitchen becomes a casual meeting point for the many US poets Roger is bringing over at this time: Saul Williams, Will Power, Sarah Jones.

One British poet who find himself there is Jacob Sam-La Rose. The young Londoner is roaming the spoken-word scene, at gigs night after night, seeing whatever he can: spoken word, MCs, hip hop artists, actors. He has always liked poetry on the page; now he's discovering what it can do on a stage, the spaces it can open up, for him as a poet, for those around him. The vibe is can-do optimistic, up for it.

On the circuit, he starts noticing the same tall poet with a hat, again and again. They start talking. Not much later, Malika is in his view too. And the two of them begin to notice Jacob: his energy, his drive. When Jacob starts coming to Malika's house, a bond forms. *Are you up for running workshops?*

Around the corner from Malika, in Brixton, a new literature organisation has been setting up, offering courses in writing development. Spread the Word. Malika gets hold of their first brochure. She signs up for pretty much every course they offer. Poetry. Fiction. Short stories.

One of them is led by Kwame Dawes. The Ghanaian poet, actor, editor, critic and musician, who has spent most of his childhood in Jamaica, will become one of the biggest influences on her writing, and on her life. Later, people will look back at his workshop, which is running under the banner 'Afro-Style School', and say that it was a first meeting point. A chance.

When Kwame Dawes leaves, Malika and Roger feel a terrible void. *What we need is a space where people can come together. Write together, and build.* It's not much later that, over a shared meal, Roger will say: *What are we waiting for? Let's just do it.* After the second night, Patricia, Janett, Peter and the others are leaving, elated. Everyone is saying: *See you next Friday?*

Malika and Roger look at each other. They hadn't really thought beyond this point. But they say: *Okay.*

*

The numbers grow – quickly. Word spreads. It's like a secret knock. *You write poetry? Come down!*

People are hearing it all over town. Like the young law student Sundra Lawrence, who has just moved into publishing, looking for something more creative to do with her life. Back then there is no online community she can easily tap into, no way to follow or sign up. All she can think of is to try and get to a poet she has seen to be very active locally: Anjan Saha. They meet; he tells her about Kitchen. It clicks immediately. She marvels at the professionalism of something she thought people treated like a hobby. She thinks: *Gosh, I need to up my game.*

Or the editor and journalist Denise Saul, who's just decided to make writing fiction the focus of her life. Her local library recommends a workshop led by Jacob Sam-La Rose. She misses it, but the librarian gives her Jacob's email address. Denise sends him some of her work. *Come to Kitchen*, he says.

At the first session she attends he suggests that, really, her short story should be a poem. Denise has no interest in writing poetry. But she considers this. Over the next year and a half, she will become one of the collective's most active members. Writing, performing, *living* poetry.

The Kitchen quickly finds its own rhythm: they read poetry, they write poetry, they critique each other's work. Roger will go: *Let's see.*

Patricia has gathered all her courage to bring in this poem she has written about visiting her grandfather in Jamaica. Roger takes out his pen, and begins: *Right, don't need that.* Patricia shivers.

Don't need that.
Don't need that.
Don't need that.

Patricia looks at him. *Oh my god. That's half the poem gone!*

But she makes the changes anyway. Like everyone in the collective, she trusts the process, whoever is critiquing the poem. Because it's only ever the poem, never the person. And there is only one aim: to make the poem as good as it can be. This dedication is Kitchen's heartbeat. They realise that there is always room to improve your craft, *no matter who you are.* Patricia will go back to her piece with a new confidence. 'Granddad' will move with her, performed in the UK and abroad, one of her dearest pieces.

It doesn't take long for Kitchen to have something to work towards: the group has been invited to perform, as a collective, at the Bug Bar in Brixton. Malika asks them to choose three pieces each, refine and practice them. Know them inside out. Everyone is determined to have stage presence for the night. Everyone wants the work to be as tight as it can be.

At the margins of the establishment, a bunch of poets are carving out a space. To many of them, it feels like they're being given a new kind of permission: to write about things that come from a really painful place. To speak for themselves. Of themselves. And they know: Literature is not entertainment; it's a form of social change. This belief charges the room, like electricity. The response to the injustice ingrained in the system that produces the country's literary culture is a bedroom in Brixton. Every Friday.

September 12, 2001. The Bug Bar, Brixton. The night is sold out: two hundred people fill the room. Patricia kicks things off. It's her first time on a stage since leaving school. Stepping up to the microphone she can feel her nervousness, but it fades with the reassurance of her fellow Kitchen members in the audience. She begins.

One after the other, the poets step up to the microphone, not just reading, but performing. Many are doing this for the first time in their lives, reaching deep into themselves; sharing with generosity, and with a new and still unfamiliar confidence. There is an undeniable, inescapable energy about the collective that night. It floats from the stage, touching those listening.

One of them is an American woman called Maya. She comes over straight after. *Guys. I want to book you, as a collective, for one of our shows. It's at the Battersea Arts Centre.* Hot on the heels of its first-ever outing, Kitchen has its second gig in the bag.

Afterwards they stand together, a little delirious from what happens when you perform poetry to an audience and the audience catches on. *What's next?*

TWO

It's 2004, and Bernardine Evaristo decides it's time. The novelist, poet, playwright and academic, who will win the 2019 Booker Prize, contacts the literature department of Arts Council England, and urges them to investigate the lack of diversity in British poetry. They offer the funding. A full year of quantitative and qualitative research follows.

When *Free Verse* comes out, what matters is a single digit: only one percent of the poetry published by major UK publishing houses is by Black and Asian poets. One percent.

*

The collective, meanwhile, is meeting religiously. Whatever else is happening, somehow everyone manages to make the time, on a Friday night, for Kitchen. And no one wants the sessions to end. Afterwards, the poets get entangled in long conversations, moving slowly, or not at all: Malika will draw the curtain of her room, and there they still are, outside on the pavement, talking poetry.

Often, they will head out for a meal together. See a movie at the Ritzy. Seek out a late-night performance, or a gig. Some of these Fridays don't end until Saturday morning, on 4 a.m. night buses, heads ringing with a new kind of fellowship.

By now, Malika and Roger have brought in Jacob – who's been supporting the two, helping out wherever he can – to lead the collective alongside them.

During the week, the poets have started to buddy up, setting goals for each other, checking in through an informal but highly effective system that makes sure the work continues. Malika buddies with a poet she goes back with a long time, through Spread the Word courses, Afro-Style School and now Kitchen. Karen McCarthy Woolf happens to move into a flat up the road from her, just as the two are pushing their drive, their mutual admiration and their work ethic to the next level.

*

When Malika's beloved aunt – the person she grew up with in Brixton – passes away, her loss is bigger than anything. She knows she cannot run Kitchen for a while. *Shall I just give people the keys?* But the collective steps up immediately. They meet in other people's houses for a while. At some point, Be Manzini – poet, spoken-word artist, filmmaker – hosts them for a stretch at Stratford Circus, where she works. The approach is flexible. An email makes the rounds, often on the day: *See you at the Southbank Centre later. Down in the foyer.* A group of poets, huddled wherever there is space.

A young Inua Ellams finds his way to the collective around this time. Born in Nigeria, he moves to London aged eleven, starts performing in cafés in 2003. Working on his craft at the Kitchen table, he has no way of knowing that he will become one of the country's foremost poets, performers and playwrights, moving from the Theatre Royal Stratford East to Glastonbury, from Edinburgh to the National Theatre.

At the Albany, Bernardine sits down with Emma Hewett, director of Spread the Word. The findings of the Free Verse report are still in their minds. An idea is taking shape. The two women discuss a programme, something that will prepare Black and Asian poets to go further, and be taken on by the big publishing houses. A mentoring scheme. When the job description to run the scheme goes up, it is seen by a Buenos Aires-born writer, academic and activist, who is working on a range of national mentoring programmes in the UK at the time. *This sounds interesting.* She applies. Soon after, Nathalie Teitler takes up the role that will become her life for the best part of a decade. The Complete Works will

12

do more to bring new voices into the UK poetry mainstream than anything has done before or since. To create careers, transform lives.

*

Meanwhile, Peter Kahn has returned to Chicago. Supercharged by Kitchen, he takes spoken-word education in the high school setting to the next level. But he thinks back to his time in London a lot, misses Kitchen (in his two years in the UK, he did not miss a single session). Roger, ever the instigator, says to him: *Why don't you start your own?* As much as he benefitted in London, he wants people to benefit here. He reaches out to some old friends; they start meeting in his apartment. The Chicago chapter is born.

In Chicago and London, Peter and Jacob are coming up with a new concept: let's put poets into inner-city schools, as poets-in-residence, and get them to excite teenagers about poetry. Let's bring the kids together for a community building day, where the teams split up, learn with each other, become friends. Give them confidence, so they can grow, develop, improve their English. Let's do it all on the Kitchen ethos. At the end, let's bring them together, at a grand venue, with parents, teachers and poets, and let them compete in a celebration, a full-on poetry slam, where everyone gets to show their best work. Malika, Roger, Sundra and others get involved as poet coaches. Kitchen feeds energy and enthusiasm into the system. The London Teenage Poetry Slam will run for seven successful years.

A new incentive is quickly added: the highest-scoring team of the year receives an invitation to Chicago. When Malika's team wins, it's a Kitchen affair: a whole group goes over, performing at the Oak Park River Forest Slam Show, in the Silver Room at the legendary Green Mill. Peter hooks them up with work in schools, introduces them to local poets. People stay in living rooms, on couches, wherever there is space.

*

Zoom out of the US, and back into Europe: Amsterdam. Patricia Foster is walking along the canals when she stops, startled, in front of a huge billboard ad that carries her name. She has been invited to perform as part of an event at the Paradiso, billed as Double Talk, combining poetry and hip hop. She shares the bill with the US poet Sharrif Simmons. Patricia looks at the ad. She can't help but acknowledge a new reality: *This is my life now. This is what's going to happen.*

Walking with her in Amsterdam that day is another poet, Nick Makoha.

Born in Uganda, he flees the country with his mother as a result of the civil war during the Idi Amin dictatorship. Lives in Kenya and Saudi Arabia, settles in London. He is a frustrated writer. His poetry feels like chewing cardboard to him. He wants more, needs more. Malika and Roger see this in him, the way they see it in many. *Just come to Kitchen.*

He does, and becomes one of its fastest-developing members. He takes part in the Chicago exchange once, twice. His writing takes leap after leap. At some point, Peter says to him: *You should take some responsibility.*

The collective has reached a juncture. For several years, Malika, Roger and Jacob have carried the collective, rotating leadership in a way that worked for the three of them. When Malika, always hands-on, is overwhelmed with other things, Roger steps up. Jacob carries it for a full year. Between them they keep the group going. But it's starting to have a draining effect on their work, their creative process, their lives.

Jacob is about to start Roundhouse Poets, and will be putting more and more energy into youth-facing programmes, eventually founding and running the widely admired Barbican Young Poets. Roger is running Spoke Lab, mixing poetry and theatre, among countless other things. For Malika, the invitations and commissions keep coming in.

How do you run a poetry collective that keeps growing, keeps demanding more? When do you admit that you need a break if you want to keep going?

The founding members decide to sit the group down. Nick still has Peter's words about taking responsibility ringing in his ears. Others know what, deep down, he knows: *We are kind of like spoilt children, mummy brings the books, daddy brings the workshops.*

Roger is straightforward with the group that night: *You guys need to start taking responsibility for this thing. You can't just keep receiving, and not giving.* It's not meant in a bad way – everyone knows. *We need to pass the baton on.*

Nick steps forward.

*

When the first round of The Complete Works is being published, in an anthology by Bloodaxe Books, Bernardine writes in her introduction: *We hope that in the next few years others will complete full-length collections, too, and that when they come knocking, the gatekeepers will at last open their doors.* Malika Booker. Denise Saul. Roger Robinson. Karen McCarthy Woolf. Nick Makoha. Five of the ten poets in the book are members of Malika's Poetry Kitchen. Something has started to connect.

With Nick in the lead, the collective starts to change in practical ways. To ease the burden on workshop leaders, they move to three shorter terms per year, ten sessions each. When a minimal subscription fee is introduced, some eyebrows are raised: money was never meant to come near Kitchen. But a convincing case is made: subs are a way to assure commitment at a time when the collective is going through a period of transformation.

There is space for sixteen poets. Everyone else is on a waiting list. If you're in, you're committing to attend at least six out of ten sessions. Other changes will have more direct impacts: Nick starts to integrate sessions on career development, often placed at the beginning of the term. He starts to ask: *What do you want to be as a writer? How can we develop as professionals?* He introduces the discipline of working towards something and – the hardest of all – finishing it.

*

Nii Ayikwei Parkes is at the Bug Bar at Kitchen's first-ever gig. The poet and writer has just arrived from Ghana, his first poetry pamphlet in his bag, and is keen to build his community. He talks to Malika afterwards. *Come to Kitchen,* she says. He does, and stays for about a year. At some point, Roger has a go at him about his poetry not being grounded in reality. At the end of that session, Nii gives him his pamphlet to read. A week later Roger apologises. *I get it now; you have a thing – you're different.* It's the beginning of a long and fruitful relationship.

Together with J. A. Parkes, Nii is hatching a plan: they want to found a publishing house. Poetry and prose, with a focus on new writers that have potential. But above all, Nii wants his books to be affordable. Over the next decade, flipped eye publishing will grow and develop into one of the country's most important small publishers of poetry.

Nii doesn't set out to publish members of Kitchen, but he happens to be in a place where he can see them, just as some of them are reaching the point they have been working towards for so long: their work is ready. Nii is discerning – *I wouldn't publish my own mother if I didn't feel her work had merit* – and he can see how good these poets are. As he enters into the writer–editor relationship, he notices straight away that the authors display a great openness to having their work questioned. Kitchen has prepared them well.

Roger Robinson's first collection *Suitcase* comes out on flipped eye in 2005. The same year Inua Ellams publishes his pamphlet *13 Fairy Negro Tales*. Jacob Sam-La Rose follows a year later, with his pamphlet *Communion*. Karen McCarthy Woolf with *The Worshipful Company of Pomegranate Slicers*. Malika's *Breadfruit*, the result of many intense sessions between her and Nii at the British Library, arrives in 2007; also Denise Saul's poetry debut, *White Narcissi*. The message flipped eye is sending to other members of the collective is a powerful one: *If you want to be published by us, your work needs to be up there. Keep working on it. Get it to the right place.*

The pamphlets shift the goalposts. When Peter Kahn asks Nii if he would consider publishing an anthology of Kitchen poets, he doesn't have to think twice. He knows there are poets in the collective who aren't quite ready for a pamphlet, and this is the way to get them started in the editing process, trigger them to working toward something more substantial. Get them onto the page.

There's a call-out for poets to send their best five pieces. Roger, Jacob, Malika and Peter select. Nii edits, without favour. The first result of this is a pamphlet; the second a book. *A Storm Between Fingers* comes out in July 2007, with a foreword by Kwame Dawes: *Malika's Kitchen is a literary movement whose impact on British poetry will be felt for a long time to come.*

Slowly, and still largely unseen from the mainstream, change is starting to travel through the system. Wherever you look, Kitchen members have started to write their own stories.

THREE

It's 2009 and the poet, performer and presenter Jill Abram roams the London poetry scene, hungry for good work, for new connections. She sees Denise Saul perform her poetry, and is deeply affected. Afterwards, the poet tells her: *I'm a member of Malika's Poetry Kitchen.*

The story repeats itself. Again and again Jill hears it, from some of the best poets she encounters; reads it in programmes for festival and events: *I'm a member of Malika's Poetry Kitchen.* She wonders: *What is this collective for women of colour?* (She doesn't at this point know that Kitchen is not restricted to women, nor to writers of colour.) She starts to make enquiries.

Not much later, Jill is at a performance workshop in Wandsworth. The tutor:

Malika Booker. They click instantly. Another session follows, and then an email: *We think you should join Kitchen.*

When Jill first sits down at the table – a bit nervous, a bit unsure – she has no way of knowing that she will become the longest-running leader of Malika's Poetry Kitchen to date, longer than even Malika.

That first session, she thinks: *I can't believe I am considered worthy to join.*

*

Leeds, Yorkshire. From a tiny office on King's Avenue, in a run-down part of the city, Jeremy Poynting is running the country's most important independent publisher of Caribbean and Black British writing. The operation publishes twenty books a year, with three hundred authors from twenty countries under its belt – all on a shoestring. Bernardine Evaristo's first ever book, *Island of Abraham*, a work of poetry, is published by Peepal Tree. Kwame Dawes' *Progeny of Air*, the book that will win the 1994 Forward Prize for Best First Collection. Roger Robinson's *Suckle*, and then his *A Portable Paradise*.

Jill is eager to start her second year with the collective. Every day she checks her email for the new term times, but there's nothing. The schedule should have been with the members a good while ago. But: nothing. She knows how busy Malika is at this point. A thought crosses her mind. *Perhaps I could help out with the organisational side of things? It's only a bit of admin.*

For years people have been saying to Malika: *You need a book. How can you not have a book by now?* But Malika doesn't want to bring out anything until she feels she's ready. *You need to find your voice,* Kwame Dawes used to write in the margins of her drafts. *Who the hell is this voice?* she keeps wondering. Malika knows she needs to concentrate on her writing. *I need to work on me, if I want to finish what I need to do ...*

At a book launch at Tate Modern, Jill goes up to Malika and asks her, straight out: *Do you want me to take over Kitchen?* Malika doesn't hesitate. The following day, Jill heads to Malika's flat, down the road from hers. They talk. When she leaves, she has taken on the collective. *It's just a bit of admin,* she thinks.

Malika finally cracks the poem she has been writing about her grandmother – the poem that will become 'Pepper Sauce' – and something starts to open up for her. The manuscript for a collection is coming together. She tackles vast emotional, historical subjects, with a sharp lens on specific human situations. Kwame Dawes, by now Poetry Editor at Peepal Tree Press, reads it. He tells Malika: *You can send your work out to anybody if you want to, but I'd love to publish you.*

When *Pepper Seed* comes out in 2013, it is longlisted for the OCM Bocas Prize and shortlisted for the Seamus Heaney Centre Prize. The collection that took Malika eleven years to publish brims with the confidence of someone who has had the strength to wait.

*

One year later; a Tuesday in November. The Lost Theatre, Vauxhall. Ten current members of Malika's Poetry Kitchen are on stage, performing poetry to a packed room. Patricia and Janett take the stage – ten years on from when they first crouched in Malika's bedroom.

The anniversary event is Jill's first major undertaking for Kitchen: she pitches the idea, produces it, hosts the night. Kitchen alumna Aoife Mannix headlines alongside Inua and Malika. As Malika's slot comes closer, she's nowhere to be seen. As so often in these days, she has double-booked herself. Jill is nervous.

But Malika arrives – just in time. The night is a triumph. A sense of celebration fills the air. And the new leader has an inkling that Kitchen is something she can do things with.

But the numbers are dwindling. Many long-term members are moving on, have other commitments. Children who demand that they be home on Friday nights. Jill decides to have a recruitment session, one of several to come, a taster: Kitchen meets the poet, the poet meets Kitchen. Usually, they click instantly.

Timid European voices. Poetry in a still-broken second (or third) language. Working-class mothers. The precariously underemployed. Queer Black men. The borders of what is seen as the outskirts of the *poetry world* are constantly shifting.

The collective does not draw lines. If you're on the margins, trying to get in, you're welcome. Whatever the margins are. Kitchen doesn't judge. The secret knock is being heard by those who need to hear it.

The early members stay close. Roger, up to his ears in other work, says: *If it's for Kitchen, I'm there.* Nick leads sessions whenever he can. Every summer, Peter comes over from Chicago, stays with Malika, and spends time with his old

Kitchen friends. He always leads a session. There is an urge, deep inside everyone who has benefitted from Kitchen – in whichever way, big or small – to give back.

If Jill needs Malika, she is there, helping to make decisions, advising on concerns, supporting in whichever way she can. Often, they operate as a team: when Spread the Word loses their funding and moves to the Albany in Deptford (without space for Kitchen) they head next door to the Poetry School, where Malika was a student, and now often teaches. When they leave they have secured Kitchen a new long-term home.

Every term, Malika leads at least one session (people joke that if she doesn't, they will take her name off the masthead). Whenever she does, she thinks: *The diversity in the room. The energy. The different voices. Nowhere else would this motley crew sit together like this. These guys come from all walks of life. And this poetry thing holds them together.*

And a small pain travels through her: *Why am I not teaching here every Friday?*

Jill doesn't set out to put her own stamp on the collective, but works to continue Malika's legacy. It becomes clear straight away that she has the same unwavering spirit, and the same ability to bring people in, to bring people together. She never leads a session, but she runs the show with a new efficiency, and the old generosity and care. When she meets the US poet Gregory Pardlo at the Aldeburgh festival; she doesn't so much ask as instruct him to lead a session when he's in London next. To Katrina Naomi, she says: *If you ever happen to be in London on a Friday, email me.*

By now, it's happening the other way round, too. Poets approach her, or Malika, to say: *I want to lead a session.* At Ledbury, Nasser Hussain says: *I'll come down from Sheffield for it, no problem.* When Speaking Volumes, Renaissance One and others have poets over from elsewhere in the world, they think of Kitchen, and contact Jill. Shivanee Ramlochan. Kei Miller. Mona Arshi. Anthony Joseph. Tania Hershman. Fiona Benson. The list of guest poets keeps growing. A new ecosystem is starting to evolve around Kitchen.

On Fridays, Jill will sometimes look at the group – feverishly writing, despite the day and the hour and busy weeks and hectic lives – teaching each other; connecting with guests in completely unexpected ways. And she thinks: *I've brought these people together.* It brings her more joy than most things, even her own writing.

Sometimes, Malika will joke: *Whenever I think I might be rid of this thing, someone else picks it up and keeps it going!*

Outside, the landscape is changing. In 2015, Karen McCarthy Woolf is short-listed for the Forward Prize for Poetry. A year later, when Kei Miller wins the prize for Best Collection, the Director of the Forward Arts Foundation, Susannah Herbert, looks at pictures Jill has posted: Kitchen members celebrating with Kei at a bus stop. That's when the significance of his win hits Susannah. After a suggestion from future member Maisie Lawrence, she signs up Malika to chair the judges for the 2016 Forward Prizes. The following year Malika herself is shortlisted for Best Poem. The poetry prize circuit has started to take note.

Kayo Chingonyi's appointment as poetry editor of *The White Review* stands as an example for a new drive, increasingly visible across the board, to diversify the pages of magazines and journals; to bring what's printed in line with what's actually happening in poetry right now.

In the US, the poet and educator Terrance Hayes and Peter Kahn have been playing around with a new form. The Golden Shovel started with a poem of the same name, which Terrance wrote to honour one of his literary heroes, Gwendolyn Brooks: you borrow a line, or lines, from someone else's writing, and use each word as the line ending in your new poem. A project is taking shape. *What if we created a book full of Golden Shovels, in honour of Gwendolyn?* Ravi Shankar and Patricia Smith join as co-editors.

Peter plans a launch for the book in London. Malika gives him contacts, Nick helps out. Terrance and Patricia say they're up for participating. Deep down, Peter knows that it has to be a celebration of Kitchen as well. Not just because there are so many members in the book, but one wouldn't be there without the other.

If it wasn't for Kitchen, I wouldn't have co-edited this book. Wouldn't have created my position in Chicago. Wouldn't be nearly as good a poetry educator. Wouldn't be coming to London every summer. Wouldn't have my own book coming out soon…

When they arrive at the British Library that night, Malika and Roger come prepared to read their Golden Shovel poems, and enjoy a night with old friends. The Knowledge Centre of the Library is packed. Terrance Hayes thunders his *American Sonnets for my Past and Future Assassin* from the podium. Peter then asks Malika and Roger to join him on stage. Malika is confused. She looks at Roger: *Why is he inviting us up? This is a Golden Shovel event.* Peter has a simple request for the audience: *Stand up, anybody who has ever been influenced by Malika's Poetry Kitchen.*

Huge swathes of the audience jump up straight away. Then others. Then more. Malika's eyes widen. All over the auditorium, people are getting out of their seats. Soon, those still sitting are the minority. She is speechless.

What's standing in the Knowledge Centre of the British Library that night is a kind of gratitude. It's also a kind of pride. Malika thinks: *But it's just this thing we did in my kitchen!*

Roger doesn't often go back as far, or reach as deep; that night he does. He talks about the early days. The days before Kitchen. About the struggle, *when no one wanted to hear from us*. He nearly breaks down, talking. *No one wanted to hear from us!*

Afterwards, people come towards each other, shake hands, and hug. Stories are exchanged. Memories.

A realisation begins to spread: For everyone it has touched directly – those sitting at the Kitchen table, working on craft, building confidence – the collective has touched others still, more gently.

Malika still can't believe it. *This is what we've done?*

*

January 2020. The Wallace Collection, Marylebone. Roger Robinson is sitting at a table with his wife. He is here to enjoy himself, appreciate and celebrate the power of poetry.

When, four months earlier, news breaks that *A Portable Paradise*, his third collection, has been shortlisted for the T. S. Eliot Prize, a wave of unmediated joy travels through the poetry world. It's a shortlist of the time: urgent, honest, unafraid. The chair of the judges, John Burnside, calls them *some of the finest and most fearless poets working today.*

What erupts the moment he says Roger Robinson's name is nothing short of a roar. Those standing in front of Malika are deafened by her scream.

Roger, instinctively, looks behind himself to see who they've called. It's too ingrained still, even now: the feeling that this is not for them, can't be for them.

Roger. His wife nudges him. *Roger, it's you.*

All eyes are on the tall man with the hat. He doesn't move.

It's you!

When he gets up he has neither his book nor his glasses. *Where is Roger's book? Does anyone have Roger's book?* Once on stage, he shakes the shock. *This is a win for a small press that works very, very hard; thank you Peepal Tree Press for giving a home to my writing.* A wave of applause. *Support small presses when you can.* He pauses a moment. Then: *This is for Malika's Kitchen. This is for The Complete Works. This is for Latinx poets. This is for Apples & Snakes. This is for Spread the Word. This is for everyone who ever looked like me who's stepped up to a microphone on the open mic scene and wondered if they will like it. This is for all those people. Thank you so much for this prize.*

In the audience, Malika Booker is crying. Denise Saul is crying. Jill Abram is crying. Nathalie Teitler is crying.

Those who have been with Roger from the beginning know that this poet has held on to his own voice, has trusted and believed in it, against all the odds, for over twenty years now. This is his reward.

Afterwards, the shortlisted poets seek him out. There's appreciation, admiration, love. Sharon Olds, a presiding spirit for both Roger and Malika, comes over. They hug, and hug again. When Roger returns from doing press interviews, Jay Bernard makes a determined beeline and flings their arms around him.

Bernardine, Roger. Within the space of a few months, the UK's two most important literary prizes in their respective genres – the Booker for fiction, the Eliot for poetry – have been awarded to two Black British writers.

It couldn't happen overnight, and it didn't come from nothing. It was made possible by a multi-layered, interconnected support system that was created because it was necessary; because nothing like it existed; by inspired individuals, often without a masterplan or much assistance, financial or otherwise. It sustained itself, through itself, for decades, quietly weaving its web of companionship. Teaching community in the truest sense.

And at the epicentre of this sits a poetry collective that began with a bunch of poets sitting together in a bedroom in Brixton.

As the poets celebrate Roger's win, he says to Jill: *I want to come and lead a session for Kitchen.*

The poems

At the corner of New Market and East

Allison Lindner

I watched the operating table dead give the last salute to his comrades
I watched the hydroelectric dam get sold for economic development policies
I watched cassava bread turn back into dusty cassava flour
I watched the last soviet shirt jack return to a soil which nursed cotton seeds
I watched the govahment boots give the final kick to the national service and
      to young men now idle with ambition
I watched this before the clocks switched back for good so I could only play
      tennis until 6 instead of 7

Because I was sitting on Daddy's shoulders at the corner of New Market and East
(right before they closed down the top half of East going towards Lamaha
and before Desmond turned from Hoyte into Persaud)
I watched as purple Sanata cotton drove by on a hearse that made it to the
      end of a gas station queue and blackouts became fewer and then few
Because even a child could recognise the death of the Kabaka

Decline past tense: 'say'

Anna Doležal

a pile of bodies they said
lay deep below the best boletus mushrooms

a pile of bodies you said
that were never found

a pile of bodies we said
might be discovered when excavations
are underway

a pile of bodies it said
lay bloated on the intertidal zone

a pile of bodies she said
but no survivors

a pile of bodies he said
the search has ended

a pile of bodies you said
and how did you react?

a pile of bodies I said
is something I have never seen

This is a Prayer

Anne Enith Cooper

This is a prayer for the dispossessed, for the fallen and we've all fallen sometime, for the children beaten or starved by their parents, left with bruises and swollen bellies, for the children abandoned outside a church or supermarket, for those parents to heal the hurt that made them that way.

This is a prayer for the dispossessed, for the fallen and we've all fallen sometime, for the children in war zones, dust between their toes, for the children that flee war zones and drown in the sea or lie dead, face down in the sand, for those who lied to start those wars, those who financed those wars.

This is a prayer for the dispossessed, for the fallen and we've all fallen sometime, for the children living in poverty, shoes too tight squeezing their feet, for the children without a place to call home, sleeping with cockroaches and rats, for those that value shares more than foodbanks and homeless shelters.

This is a prayer for the dispossessed, for the fallen and we've all fallen sometime, for the children who have lost parents to tragedy, for the children trafficked and sold into slavery, shivering alone, scarred and don't know who to trust, for those for whom cash has stolen their souls.

This is a prayer for the dispossessed, for the fallen and we've all fallen sometime, for the children that die from wounds, bleeding out in playgrounds and alleys, on the street, for the children living in fear and confusion, taking up knives and guns, for those who failed to give them guidance or opportunity.

This is a prayer for the dispossessed, for the fallen and we've all fallen sometime, for the children who march out and march up, for the children who strike on Fridays, for those who support them and for the earth that holds us when we fall, that sustains us and succours us, crying *now is the time.*

Fire

Aoife Mannix

I break into my neighbour's house.
It is derelict since she burnt it down last summer
in a fit of fire engines and exploding windows.
There are letters piled in large stacks.
My son stands behind me. We both know
this place is haunted. I examine the pipes,
the whistle of their reflected sorrow
rattling in the walls. I am sorry I stopped
writing to you. I know you dreaded a phone call
but somehow your theories on how to avoid
other people's dreams became personal.

I wanted you to listen to white rooms
waiting for knives. You locked yourself up
in a French house on a cliff
claiming you were rehearsing.
I clung on by my fingernails.
Days of tedious pain.
Now the children play in the cups of daffodils.
My son wants to hang his dreamcatcher
in the window so he can hold on to the dark
that slips through his fingers.

We are burglars playing at arson.
My neighbour has disappeared.
My skin is scabbed with ghosts.
I wake to watch my son sleeping.
The perfect bow of his lips.
He is yawning in the language of those
who don't know where this real life begins.
You never could deal with insomnia,
death, the suffering of strangers you once loved.

Tulips

Arji Manuelpillai

I can hear her in the kitchen, talking on the phone
the way a daughter only talks to her father, a voice
soft at the seams, familiar, woven with history
like fossils uncovered along the Northumberland coast.
They discuss important things like vinyl flooring
or shelves or how they will plant tulips this winter
though he knows he'll probably never see them bloom.
That night, in bed, she cannot stop crying.

In kneepads and old khakis, weeks later
soil-soaked hands clamber in bushes, bury
green-fingered secrets at the base of a great oak
planting tulips as he teaches and I catch her,
behind his watering can, for a second, staring
as a daughter only stares at her father
like he is the sky and she is a boat below it.
That night she asks me *who's gonna tell me it'll be alright?*

It's Saturday, *Strictly* night, he is stretched out
sipping chocolate mousse, batting tales of Nigeria
to his daughter who reaches for his stories
like feathers from a falling bird, he laughs,
she wipes mousse from his shirt, exchanging a glance
from when she was nine, with a grazed knee, hobbling
to a man who could make the ground say it was sorry.
I hope so, he says as the credits roll. *I would love to see them grow.*

It's a year since he passed. Spring in our tiny flat,
she is consoling our heartbroken neighbour,
the neighbour sobs into her shoulder, she listens,
her forehead a crinkled crash-mat, nodding, speaking
with tender voice, each word a bird, nursed
and released from her mouth, the rain outside is falling,
our neighbour shakes his head like I am shaking mine
wondering where her kindness comes from
and there, on the balcony, tulips, tall as I have ever seen.

The Last Compass Point

Be Manzini

His hands remember fighting for food
searching through bones for loved ones
cupping Papa's chest tightly to ease the bleeding
until his heart stopped

waving goodbye to Sierra Leone.
It is the first time Mohammed has seen snow.
He spreads sun-blackened hands on the ivory blanket.
A cold freedom comes from this movement.

Three weeks ago, he arrived at a locked room
two immigration officers, one pale interpreter
and Mohammed, the last compass point, facing east,
facing fear. He knelt as the trinity talked,

unable to clutch at their words.
Ungloved, his hands can survive
a freezing British welcome at Christmas.
Those hands, outstretched, searching for Allah.

In varying dilutions

Bernadette Reed

I   When it comes to water,
        sound drowns.

II   The river is in the house
        is in the river. It's futile to take sides.

III   Heaven is a drop of water.
        Hell, contrary to popular opinion,
        is freezing.

IV   In the language of angels,
        the word for God is Duw.

V   Tears and loathing
        may devour what love leaves,
        but thirst will come first.

VI   Sublime soda stream
        of consciousness.

VII   Your smile is an ocean.
        It soothes the horizon.

VIII When the lava at Hilo
        crashed into the ocean
        neither was put out.

IX   Feel the sound.
        Through the ground;
        silent as the ocean.

X   Without water
the heart wouldn't start.

XI   The rhino's hide was moved
by the waterhole.

XII   Our skin is generally
watertight.

XIII   Returning to Eden
is climbing a waterfall.

Birthday

(after Dorothea Tanning)

Cath Drake

Alone, half-dressed, barefoot, I'm turning circles,
staring down the corridors, trying out the views

of so many doors, windows, open, half-open, ajar,
their dazzling glass reflecting, distorting;

a new angle with every turn, my belly shifting,
focus / refocus, lurch forward / sideways:

glimpses of wildflowers on a sill / the back
of a beaded dress in flight / belting rain / the soft end

of an argument / a well-dressed man crooning
at a kitchen sink / smoke wafting / a hand

reaching for another / music and lamps switching
on / off. Spinning on my heels, I'm telling myself

to start again, start again, don't worry, this time
just take a door, one door, every direction

is as little known as the next. Button up, mirror check,
straighten, fling on your aqua jacket, best boots,

scoop up the mess on your desk into a briefcase
and take an exit grandly, beautifully, slowly, step, step,

step, step because doors lead to windows, lead to
doors, lead to more windows and reflections multiply.

Grimhilde's eclipse

Charlotte Ansell

When no one contradicts my protests
I turn to imperfect mirrors, ask for lies.
Who is the fairest of them all?

Gives too many hollow replies;
frustrated, I stay here and cling.
My eldest has no need to try;

if admiration became leers I would spring
she-wolf to protect her. Have I held to her lips
a poisoned apple while doves sing?

As buds bloom on her chest would I snip
them back? The shadows call.
She is sunrise to my moon, I am eclipsed,

my body collapsed upon itself; a sinkhole.
I lack the grace for crow's feet, laughter lines,
Not yet ready to become invisible.

I'm imprisoned by reflections, while my girl shines.

Rebirth

Christina Fonthes

This is for you, Black Girl
You who came into this world with nothing but your broken brown skin
and a zinc bucket full of salt water

This is for you, Black Girl
You who were told that your hair was too kinky, too coily, too tight, too
Black, too thick, too ugly. For them to love you

This is for you, Black Girl
You who were told to close your legs when uncle came to visit, only for him to
be waiting around the corner when your mum went to her cleaning job in the
mornings

This is for you, Black Girl
You who were told that you are not enough
that you can't keep a man
that you can't be with a woman
that you shouldn't have had so many goddamn
children

This is for you, Black Girl
You who went to sleep hair wrapped in an ice blanket under the gaze of a
grinning moon and woke up to the sounds of police sirens and flashing lights
in a half-painted bedroom

You gave yourself a new name, Queen
Sewed it in gold and red at the hems of your tongue
doused your body in coconut oil
rinsed away the stains of self-hatred from your sinews

This is for you, Black Girl
You who made a crown
from barbed wire and dead butterfly wings

This is for you, Black Girl
You who turned your scars into poetry

This is for you
Black Girl

Return

Cyril Husbands

Scatter my remains to
Ancestral Earth
where the Harmattan
will return me
to their ephemeral
embrace and I
shall fertilise the
ground that gave me life
as the Ancestors did
before me and those
who follow will do
for The Children

At the Edge of a Terrain

Daniel Kramb

There's too much autumn now
for one life
to still see

my word-wrapped
worldlessness

like a wound
stretching out my skin:

I can no longer think in this country.

Shrink-sealed sphere. A clinic cold.

My outline
shrivels

like a flower
blooming in reverse. ❧

Ode to My Cuticles

Dean Atta

When Mum wasn't too busy, she would tend to you.
Give her boy a manicure. Cuticles, always growing,
often dry, I try to keep you moisturised and neat.

Hands that work. Grip pens. Bottles of beer.
You are open curtains to an empty window, a stage
that holds so much potential. Our fingers could

hold any colour. Now Mum is too busy to notice,
I go to a nail technician. 'You don't want colour?'
he asks. I could say yes. But don't.

Why would I add any more unwanted attention
to this body? I already have this skin.
My friends tell me of street harassment

they receive for nail varnish, lipstick or eyeshadow.
No man has commented on my nails
before or after a manicure.

I notice when you are unruly, unkempt, getting out of line.
Like when my hair or beard needs a trim.
I would go to my barber weekly but when

I did, he told me I didn't need another haircut,
even though I pay him. He holds my head so tenderly
and I miss him like I've always missed my father.

I can only go to my barber every two weeks.
This haircut is so precise, yet unremarkable.
My afro and dreadlocks got too much attention

and hands in my hair without consent.
My therapist told me I can only go to him every
two weeks. I don't pay him so I have no choice.

You are with me when I tell my therapist: I wish
a man would stay with me long enough, look at me often
enough to notice you. How I do. How she used to.

Tube Pass

Dele Meiji Fatunla

His hair braided / simple
Rows of corn / sides intricate as a cornice
He bounds out / crisp white shirt
Hidden in the wrap of a denim jacket.
He does not turn back.

He hooks his jacket by his fingers,
Slings it up on his back

Down the stairs,
Onto the platform

Waiting for a train of thought
To make me bold
When my train arrives / he is turning down
those endless passageways
where strangers and dreams collide.

Someone Walked Into A Garden

Denise Saul

He's the same one who gave us the Word and took it away when we sat in the garden where bindweeds climbed the wall. This was where we heard him count seven days into a week. We saw someone who looked like you and when she turned around, it was me talking to myself. And I have dreamt this before, someone who walked into a garden. I know it's you when I talk with the god of roses; I have dreamt this often.

Elephantine

Dorothea Smartt

Roosevelt sits in the cabin of the elephantine
digger. Imported piece by piece for the Big Ditch.
Piece by piece black men with dreams arrive,
dark hats mouldy, in the damp of constant wet.
A lot of the fellahs had water to wash wid that day.
Musty felt better than no hat a'tall.
Roosevelt, white-suited, addressed workers and engineers:
'...keep the dirt flyin' boys!' Hats hurtle in d'air!
The press took pictures of shining machines and white-suited men.

Divorce Petition to HM Court of the Family Division, Mordor, Middle-earth

Elena Lagoudi

One word to rule them all, one word to break them
One word to make them go and in the darkness take them

Listen to the way they shriek those dark riders with their horses
Each shriek a reminder of his dark kingdom
The lord of misery and destruction, lies, pain, anger, abuse and the abyss
Each memory a helpless wound a lash of a whip burning like death's kiss

Only a distant land can help, run, escape, flee, bolt, break loose
Taking my broken leg with me, my twisted arms, my torso, taking what I
    could
I left the kingdom at night, a desperate fearful flight
Looked but once behind, holding my breath please, please, please was my
    shibboleth

I took my parts with me, my head under arm, my feet, my hands
Not sure if I was walking or crawling
The territory strange and unfamiliar still, so used to the terror of his kingdom
    calling
I almost missed it once, needing the daily interaction with the darkness
To endure the light at first, as it was blinding – too much light, too much air
    and solitude
Used to the constant company of pain and terror, freedom tasted almost
    foreign and lewd

Then I started stretching, feeling again, sketching
The light, the ease, the lack of hurt
I put my body parts together again one by one, arms, torso, I put the elbows
   in place
Walking, moving, twisting my new body in awe, feeling the strange space
I started seeing again, how lovely this new land was, mystic sun, islands of
   olives and zen
But then I heard his dark riders in the borders, looking for a way into my
   newfound land
And his riders seeking, sneaking, shrieking into the night
the terror still awaits in the darkness
But
I shall not be afraid
I shall not be afraid
In my newfound land

The Carpenter

Esther Poyer

Work worn
finger blocks
stretched skin
ashy lines
arched thumb
and index
Spits out nails
hammers into
yellow pine
I ask
Did your feet
have to carry
you alone
to build
this life?
Honeydew
droplets bead
his forehead
gold coins from
a balmy sky
No, he says
I collected
these tools
while on
my way.

My Headstone Read 'Beloved Daughter'

Fikayo Balogun

It was a summer evening, the breeze turned leaves into jellyfish,
ran across grasses, and I crushed blades beneath my feet on my way to find
     love.
Love pulled me by my crown, pinned my face
to the rocky scales of the baobab tree and yanked my skirt away.
Ice wind rushed between my legs, flushing my will, my freedom
through my mouth with every scream of
NO!!! Don't!! Please!
He slammed away, till he released his poison inside of me.
Its toxic glow exploding through my veins till my heart became a stone.
Crushed berries were my bed, dead leaves hugged my naked body,
I could feel the sting of a thousand bees between my legs
as the earth soaked up the slimy liquid dripping from my core.

'You woke the sleeping dragon with your giggle, love,' he said.
I wanted to scream, 'Don't tell me it is my fault that your mind is a sinkhole.'
I came to find love; no one warned me that men had become wolves.
I wanted to scream but my cords had lost the will for words as I watched him
zip up the murder weapon and laugh, his laughter flew ahead
of his thirsty boots as he beat a path away from my bartered soul.

I died that summer evening.
My headstone read 'Beloved daughter, she loved berries'.
I was buried deep on a wasted land with no berry trees.
The priest said I died an unholy death, like it was my fault
that no one saw that I died, long before I became dead.

The world asked me to speak, but words cannot
describe the injustice that has been dealt to my soul.
Words would buy you justice, they said.
I told them, what has been taken from me is my life
with my soul ripped from its root. I have disappeared
into oblivion, words cannot bring me back.

(The Rhetoric Of.)

Gemma Weekes

mighty white audience Present
performative   teaRs as
flat fee   price of admIttance at WOKEFEST
where blackfaced Vendors sell
inferiority programmes   dIrect from the vein
in exchange for acceptance   Leading the implored
to   a cushioned arEna where the plundered
perform   raGe so deliciously raw
all   unpaid dEbt is drowned by uproars

Home

Hannah Gordon

If the place you lived
never really loved you back,
was it still a home?

Things to Consider Before Your First Spacewalk

Harry Man

When you want to burst into bits, that
is what they call it: *space exposure.*

In fourteen seconds you pass out
from oxygen loss, you're able to

see the Earth – it is so expensive,
so hard to act without your lungs.

Beyond the cold, the spiralling Milky Way,
you will outgrow the size of yourself.

The dropping dark lights the way home.
One night is as long as a lesson in biology.

What goes up must keep going up.
A flipped lid can be a deadly weapon.

When there's nothing to hold on to
there is nothing to hold on to

On the Wall

Heather Taylor

At the edge of a rocky beach,
he rested his head on my shoulder
and we stared across the water.

His words were ones I knew
but the combination unfamiliar –
echoes of made-for-TV movies.

They came back to me:
my sick-day afternoons
sunk into the couch staring

except he didn't look as pale
or heroic as the leading man –
it was only a cough.

I repeated that phrase
his mantra become mine
as he leaned on me

to repeat the telephone call
from the clinic in even tones.
He mentioned his favorite flowers

and the party we'd plan
to laugh over his foibles
after he was gone.

I promised I wouldn't cry
and he said nothing
as he squeezed my hand.

Some Turn / To violence

Inua Ellams

In the beginning was the Word / perhaps the wrong one
Imagine / Sat scratching his head / elbows rested on a desk

wide as imagination / the creator / grouping together
patches of darkness / wondering / Does *Earth* sound right?

If the hard D of 'Land' suggests solidity and 'Water's last
syllable conjures ripples / does my name suggest me?

Is the nonsense question I attempt in a cafe / notepad
in hand / head of soil and stars / Ask its meaning and I'll turn

to humour or intrigue / In Kiswahili it means Elevate
In my father's tongue it translates to Shade / thus I was born

cool / I'll nervously say / expecting an awkward silence
to fall / which I'll rush to fill in with 'Eskimo' a pejorative term

rejected / foul / offensive / despised as the word 'Nigger'
They prefer 'Inuit' and worship an 'Inua' / a deity they say

breathes in all things / On discovery / when the fact sunk in
I snapped shut the laptop / found my twin sister Mariam

and / my chest puffed broad as desks / explained to her
my new elevation / Though we met before breath

before tongues formed / met before words / us / twin patches
of darkness / wet sparks in mother's womb / Inuits who walk

land that is water / worship a divine spirit of Alaska
one half man / one half myth / INUA / me / a god among men

I don't recall when her arm switched but her palm struck
my cheek so hard / I wondered about mortality / blushed

saw stars / crescents / crosses / and everything clicked
First comes a name / attempts at definition / a rush of blood

to sibling rivalry / Shiite / Sunni / Protestant / Catholic
Nigeria / Biafra / it's the same fucking thing

For the Young Men Popping Wheelies on Southwark Street in Late Afternoon Traffic

Jacob Sam-La Rose

One day, you will die.
    But not today. And perhaps
you have already tasted it,
    whatever endings taste of –
a mouth full of road and iron,
    the weight of something implacable
you couldn't lift yourself from under.
    Not today. Today you are brazen,
quick as a blade, wheels
    up, and threading into an HGV's path
and out again, uproarious, alive
    and testing whatever binds the rest of us
to good sense,
    whatever weights another driver's fist
with righteousness and ties us
    to our quaint and tidy appetites
and has us hook our eyes
    to pull you down and safe and anchored
to the meek and common ground.
    Today, everything lifts from you,
like the ringing of a bell in clean air.
    Like smoke.

Kaleidoscope

Jamal 'Eklipse' Msebele

The flavours of the world are sticky
sweets in Newham's pockets

Three miles from the City of London
in the womb of the East End
Newham sits on the bend of the river
pregnant with 365 languages and dialects

Bengali
    Greek
      Yoruba
     Patois
Cockney

Watching her belly swell each day
a shifting scene

Today I walk
through East Ham High Street
Travel the globe in an hour
smelling the fresh aromas of

Dhal
    Falafel
      Jollof rice
     Jerk chicken
Pie 'n' mash

I flare my nostrils to take it all in
like a hippopotamus yawning

Eatery lights flash at me
sunlight on silver and gold
I buy into them all
burning cultures on my tongue

This kaleidoscope swirl of tastes
holds nations in my mouth
as if my saliva were the oceans

Alphabet

Janett Plummer

My daughter beautifully draws four letters of her name
and each time omits the 'a'
– the boundary of her imagination.
The letter 'a' is a huge door, behind which
scary monsters lie in wait ready to attack.
'The letter "a" is a circle with a tail and it isn't scary,'
I explain to her yet again.

But it is the first letter, and if it can't be conquered
then how will she master the other twenty-five letters?
I learned to form alphabet letters long ago
reading Jif bottles, timetables and crisp packets.
Without the 'a' you couldn't write
absolute, almost, and –
almighty Lord give me strength!

My letter 'a' is an ally.
The circle with a tail
has caused tears, tantrums and stamped feet.
I have left it out, sneaked it in all to no avail,
it is greeted with pencil flinging and disgust
making me question if it's her or me?

'O's mutate into 'a's. With a swish of the tail
strong spermlike 'o's propel me forward
– to another Friday writing class.
They glare, I haven't done my homework,
and standing on stage doing clever
permutations with letters and verbs
has lost its appeal when I can't fight
the battle of the 'a' at home with her.

It's taken five months to watch her painstakingly write her name.
I know we're closer, when she forms four letters
and allows the 'a' to perch outside her name
a skew-whiff oval shape with a floaty tail.
Under my breath I find myself muttering the word Amen!

Twenty-two Months

Jill Abram

An elephant gives birth surrounded by her sisters,
their legs protect the calf while she removes the amnion,
kicks dust on him, tries to lift him with her trunk.

They circle until he rises, reaches for her. In the time
she gestated him, I could have given birth to two babies –
I spent it on the internet and endless first dates.

Lisa had two failed rounds of IVF, then two babies
born together. Elaine mourned two embryos until
Molly's arrival dried her tears. Rachel was pregnant

for just six months. Elly-Mae never saw the jungle
mural on her nursery wall, the swan mobile hanging
over her cot, teddies waiting to greet her, balloons.

She was born en caul but never suckled her mum,
feeding and breathing through tubes, rearranged
by appointment for skin-to-skin contact. A mother

elephant may carry her dead baby for days. The cows
cover the body with dirt and leaves. The whole herd
sings a grief song then falls silent.

This unexpected longing for what
I've always wished away

Jocelyn Page

The day is still and mild for January but the light is dim and we've kept the lamps on to work in our separate parts of the flat. I am starting to know what it might feel like to live without the children, although they'll be home by a quarter to five. An article for facial yoga seems worth a read, and the list of supplements Sam gave me has taken on the feel of observance: *fish oil, turmeric, glucosamine, bromelain, willow bark.* The days in between no longer need counting. I will most likely never be as strong as I am today, but I will keep at it. Something – anything – that raises the heart rate for twenty minutes each day. I have become too flexible for my own good.

What will mark the months
now, without this wretched loss?
I'm less now, and more.

The Claim

Joey Connolly

A stranger arrives at your door, wondering
if there is a place in your movement
for such a man as he: dedicated but
misled, pale

with such uncertainties the texts inspire,
educated and tangled
in education, skilled
in the failed technē of power. Sirens

festoon the horizons
like a paperchain. Inside the fire
is newly kindled and fresh shadows
open behind the old chairs;

there is little food and it's unclear what exactly
he is requesting of you. He is sincere
with a bankrupt earnest all hung up
on points of jagged protocol,

comes offering songs of sweet
self-justification; cleverly worked
concessions to limited culpability
and designs of his own

monolithic understanding. He is
a survivor: what does that mean?

Five days and counting

Joolz Sparkes

The come-hither puff of smoke
from cute, cordoned-off Friday night
pub outsiders, and that old familiar line
of crawlers stumbling into view, sends her
lurching from new boy to new boy
to taxi-bundled parties, *budge up doll,*
room for plenty more, a two-day bender of
build-up and paper-licked promises,
so-and-so's got a mate down the road
he'll fix you up, through gums tasting of
blood-rush powder, loving that trauma-bond
on Sunday with the sequinned survivors of
Saturday, troubadours searching for
24-hour off-license, *take your top off*
pass one round in back alleys and on strange
mattresses, dancing to the release of hand jobs,
mouths, then after, she's a stranger, spilling out
onto morning pavement, sad and spent a fortune,
feeling that inevitable comedown, deafened
by dawn chorus, her own *why again?*
guilt-trip song, dispersing into juice-cleansed
horizon, violent gym routine, hiding in
plain sight behind office and open-plan Monday.

Boomting

Kareem Parkins-Brown

Surely the Earth takes offence
when couples compare their love to it,
but here are my facts:

When a couple becomes their own world
Pangea happens on the face.

A jawline begins to walk to a forehead,
a cheekbone pokes its chest out.

Between blinks an eyelid reshapes subtly
like pizza dough in the air.

When we become a ball on the bed after work
you could spoon lava from the middle, too.

We centre ourselves in the universe
and ignore lives happening elsewhere.

No gravitational pull but
songs by Kelis and Ari Lennox.

Our protective layers have
grown holes over time.

We don't have significant fossils,
we have December 8ths and June 15ths.

We have fought no large-scale wars but see
how we fight over space.

If all this started with a bang that was big,
you should see my ting and how she booms.

Miss Birdie's Letter//A Coupling

Karen McCarthy Woolf

Dear Sister Weir,
Dear Miss Birdie,

> 1918 was a year of myriad feelings.
> *2018 is a troubled year, an anxious period.*
>
> *A spirit of uncertainty prevails, here and abroad.*
> *Our hearts are easily led along thorned and fearful*
>
> *paths, where light is a pinprick in the dark, strewn*
> *with visions of rubble and ruins, shaded by vast*
>
> *glass towers that splinter the sun as it falls at dusk.*
> *It is a time of barbed and hidden dealings, where*
>
> *the poor freeze and hard-edged*
> *men make fractious sport of war and killing.*

There were new hopes of peace,
as now, Dear Grandmother, there are few hopes for peace

and the realisation of peace, the tumult of battle was
and is wrought by aggrandised leaders, whose accumulated tittle-tattle

> *rattles at the gates, jangling the keys to freedom*
> *in the faces of those whose noses are kept*
>
> *close to the grindstone, whose limbs and minds*
> *are cannon fodder for those whose untruths are artfully*

transformed into the victorious tumult
of unadorned commitment to the cult of profit, where the whoops

of Allied rejoicing, war widows and orphans,
is still shamelessly exploited – as if the world might be divided among

those who fought and those who did not,
between those who favoured thought and those who did not,

heroes and heroines now had to face post-war society.
A society where heroines are trafficked and heroes displaced.

> *Where the sea is full*
> > *of things we can't atone for.*

> *Where the sea is full*
> > *of those who paid for yachts they'll never sail on*

> *Where the sea is full*
> > *of filthy rivers, awash with spinning gyres*

> *Where the sea is full*
> > *of empty water bottle tops, deep in the bellies of albatross*

> *Where the sea is full*
> > *of ghostly shanties*

> *Where the sea is full*
> > *of bones and babies*

Cloister

Katie Griffiths

The stillest rite.
     Certain
          this will be my lot.
Prayer falls close to the soil. Nothing stirs. This I set
     store by, my lost core,
          its tiny clot of cries.
What must silt over
     so I
          can finally let us rest?
What role
     for me, for love, our relics' perfect cost?

Chingola Road Cemetery

Kayo Chingonyi

Because of what it would take to visit
I visit tata's grave on Street View
in the early hours of mornings when
the edge of sleep is like the border at Kasumbalesa

where men with red eyes
police their sovereign patch,
Kalashnikovs at their sides;
gold standard of summary justice,
making, of a family, cartographers then sextons.

Our year nine biology teacher glossed succession:
the built environment
will always be exposed as a fad, given time.
And so, it has come to pass here
the Chingonyi name's resting place.

This is a picture of David (late),
and Muzanga (equally late),
and John Kanjamba (also late),

where we might find a stone
it is overgrown with long grasses
and plants designated weeds
because we've yet to lend them use.

I came to pay my respects
as my mother before me
kneeling at the exact spot
all she carried, like a bag of shopping,
dropped; its contents rolling.

On the tape she made
of his favourite songs
her voice cracks
in the act of speaking
as if the act is what loosed him
from this plane.

Let us pause to play him 'Hotel California'
let us say father and son
are driving together
along a coastal road
in an open-top feat
of mid-century automotive nous

the son rides shotgun
skipping tunes to test
the low end of the Altec Lansing
system in the back
as one track fades
another picks up the slack

a wayfarer's tune
written in a shack
on a four track
in the 70s:
guitar
a voice threaded with regret
each word a promise
that in the end
the singer could not keep.

mati lampu, jakarta[1]

Khairani Barokka

when electricity sucks itself extinguished,
and the round, inverted pop of lights and television,
A/Cs and radios going into slumber is all there is of it,
my heart twists to soothing blackout. lying on a mattress
as insect sounds boil steady, there is bodily relief.

no home until blackout. no more blackouts would mean
a loss of acceptance that things may cease working,
at random, that everyone here in the house has accepted this,
candles lit at the ready and shouts from room
to room. a blackout is a return to a quiet womb of stillness.
nothing else needs to be humming, dark-swept body still alive.

---

1 *blackout, jakarta*

London Fields

Kostya Tsolakis

we fucked through spring and summer / I'd cycle to you after work / you'd
greet me at the door in just a towel / I think your name was Rich / your room
was always in a mess / your bed was up against the open window / I loved the
silky fuzz that ringed your navel / we'd cum then lie down for a bit / two lads
naked on our stomachs / the breeze would cool the sweat off us / we'd peek
out through the half-raised blinds / the couples clinging on the grass / the
red-faced barbecuing dads / felt sad for them all wearing clothes

black star

mae

sky's
     startling
  the last sunset
   watcher

       smudged on
          mid-horizon

           half-glimpse
          half-swallowed by light's
        long waves and dark

     flutters, viscous,

       in circus

         trick inverting
           night, this mute

        figure into words
      tossed

     like a trapeze
    artist . . .

  landing

Marianne

Maisie Lawrence

Last night I awoke in the forest
and again it was on fire
Blue flames on the ends of branches

I went to a flame and asked to borrow the tree
Dancing with me tired out the little tree
The blue flame was a tiny ball
You made me blue, old shoe

So we slept together and the flame
grew small, with nothing left to feed on
A bluebell, as my eyes were
closing

When I awoke the flames were huge
The forest was just blue
Blue as a shoe, yes you

My tree was gone, the flames
dancing
I went to the blue flames
to start again

But they swayed together
in a rhythm I couldn't catch
And blew salt-ash into my
eyes

An Alternative History of Stones

Malika Booker

Let us address the stones

And you   stone   too   have   stories   to tell.

Back home   in   the woman's   hometown   village   young men gather
   stones
   in lush green bush
(to) create a circle of stones   to rest   their pots,   over hot coals
     cooking   oil down.

Yesterday   news   flew   across the net   like a soiled dove with a broken wing
   fragile bruises bloomed.
How long   had he   been seasoning   the woman up   to cook in her home
   like her house   was an oven?

O   let us address   the stones   as stones too have stories to tell.

Sir – you tell the poet stone does not burn; it may crack, or even be crushed into powder
but your answer is too late.

Stone – you speak of David toppling Goliath with his slingshot.

In the woman's village boys went into the bush armed with slingshots to pelt / birds /
break their wings / Is this where the man learnt to break   his dove's wings?

Remember poet   you say   this is a poem about stones   meanwhile   across

Facebook   the woman's friends   are stones rumbling / stones heavy

one post states *I spoke to her only last night.*
                    Death did not hint it was a stone's throw
                              to the crawling fire; in this poem honey thickens in the woman's
                    vein instead of water
boiling epidermis shrinks then splits   open and oil flows from the woman's body like boiling
          tears
     O give me more oil in my lamp keep it burning

her friends sing a choir across   Facebook   hymns to erase (thoughts of) oil in that oven
burning, burning till daybreak.

Sir, this is a poem about stones. Yes
          and you   stones have our stories too ... look at the woman's village – a nun sits
on a big stone,
          look again at the woman's village, a nun sits on a big stone
by the seashore   under the fire of sunset praying
                    for the woman trapped between a rock and a hard marriage.

Sir   Stone – is prayer a servant   of the mouth   like stones   are servants of the palm?
          Where were prayers at daybreak when   the woman needed
               O let us address the stones
as stones have their own story to tell.
The poet attempts to resurrect ... the poem attempts to resuscitate ... O let us address the
          stones.

Who what are we?

Mary Renouf

You hide your eyes
as you undress me.
And you cried your eyes
as service provides.
And because I did not pass
their test, I myself
and you yourself
are not ourselves,
nor it itself.

And medicine calls us users.

Accidental memory

Mehmet Izbudak

North side, at bus stop E
I warm my face to the sun
we promise to become lovers

God is dead they say and the heavens are empty
hers is an unchartered soul
an unfolded sheet of paper

I tell her that I can love her with kisses
I can love with words

It is early spring
the sky ice blue
the clouds grey and pink

She says that she is a surgeon and is Norwegian
fiddles with her phone
looking for signs of life

like some John the Baptist
the melancholy commute
will take me to the river

188
Thomas Stearns's bus
glides around the bend to an elegant halt

The Demoiselle Crane

Melanie Mauthner

Be pagan darling, worship river! You might
see me searching for berries and honey.
Praise solstice, water, amber, darling, praise me.
Be creedless, free, believe in magic, in flight.

Be swift to hear me feeding softly at night,
darling, in wetland and estuary, the Mersey
my wading ground. Heed me: be deft with sea.
Soak elderflower to shift blackfly and blight.

And what do I believe in? Oh my darling
in strand and shoreline, reeds and tides, kindness;
I'm the demoiselle crane who wants you crowned.

Be fearless, worship thunder my craneling,
let river lull you with wheatgrass and quietness.
Be blessed with sleep, a nest of fleece and down.

Truncated checklist for a Gothic novel

Michelle Penn

1. Gloom / decay / mystery

Shadows mass in corridors, drift the rickety stairs. Corners groan
and whispers skid while archaic rivalries hover, silhouettes imprinted
on walls, rotting the portraits, crumbling the boards. A hallway dead-
ends into stone. Beyond, a cry from an attic, laden with chains:
paper, daisy, iron.

2. Supernatural beings

They're crowded onto night boats, but the cities they flee remain
strapped to their backs, wound around their ankles. Buildings and streets
cramp their fingers, but they can't relax their grasp, they can't let go,
they're crowded onto night boats, they are noise-and-grime ghosts, human
chains above the ocean's simmering brew.

3. Curses / prophecies

History is not a chain. It is a mirror.

Hotel

Naomi Woddis

I can't smoke a joint here,
the alarm senses that sweet bass
of weed even as I start rolling.

The windows don't open,
air conditioning is a poor substitute
for the salt rush of sea air.

I press my forehead against the glass.
The double-glazing mutes the sound of traffic.
Two boys ride a bike without lights –

one, his legs dangling like a puppet,
the other, his mouth the shape of a scream
yelling vowel sounds at anyone who will listen.

When I am ready I will walk
to the water's edge, take unsure steps
over the pebbles and light up there,

joining all the solitary smokers
scattered along the shoreline.
Ahead of me the grey-blue line of sea

as I breathe the thick curlicue
of smoke into my lungs, waiting for
the day to shut its lazy eye,

grains of salt lighting up the black.
Heaven looks pretty tonight,
the stars shameless.

How a City Vanishes

Nick Makoha

All it takes is two men on a bike,
a convoy in their rear-view mirror,
some land, a shortage of visas,
the closing of embassies, a night
lowering its curtain of curfew
and some C-4 to turn a dirt highway
into a makeshift airstrip.

Out come the men in uniform
following the flare of a flashlight
towards life lurking in the long grass.
White soldiers with foreign words
that taste too much like caution,
huddled around a wireless waiting
for orders, keeping their voices down.

A war reporter, tourist and volunteer
with the same faces just cleared
a checkpoint. Said they were on safari,
hence the cameras. Tonight they will make
the weekend edition of *People*. Tomorrow
our city, or some version of it, will be as
familiar as the dark side of the moon.

Vogue

Nii Ayikwei Parkes

Some nights my sleep is vain, wants
to watch itself in mirrors, show off
its twists, its feints, its hilarious ability

to evade capture, how it dips its toes in
blue daydreams, then runs past desperate hours,
its compass north and awake, to the edge of

faded moon bliss – a cliff over which it just hangs
its legs, like kids in chairs too high for them,
singing questions into the altitude of my stillness

like a random herd of nuns or Von Trapps ambushed
by Alps green. It turns to its good left side
to watch itself twerk, checks out its abs

from the front, contemplates a Periscope® stream
by the backlight of an Android®. I've tried
everything sensible adults do to drift off – yes,

ev. ery. thing. I've had to go back to being a boy,
up in that bunk bed, chattering wild dreams down
to my brother until we wake up in the morning

astonished that we slept – like when I'm in love,
whispering across pillows. Some nights my sleep wants
company and it won't settle its vogueing self for less.

Ashes and Dust

Orishanti

Hell yeah I refuse to die
Old, bitter and cussed;
Filled with the taste of ashes and dust,
Creaking with decades of emotional rust,
To my own life, utterly lost ...
so whatchoo gonna do about it, motherlover?

No way I'm gonna be like my father-land,
Too often ruled by cruel and capricious men
Who gained earthly power
But lost dey very souls –
if you gamble with the devil, you better do it for love!

Won't end up like my mother-board neither
Whose Operating System got tricked
By Trojan horses; the ghosts in the machine
Hi-jacked control of the cortex, hacking through
Backdoors spawned at the dawn of the Matrix.
Time to fix the System and learn to ride the quantum vortex ...

Forget about acting like my wicked stepsisters
Who filled with vanity, envy and lust,
Not to mention stupidity, greed and wrath,
Worked real hard to make my life miserable –
dem bitches ain't got what it takes to walk a mile in my shoes!

Mos def I ain't like my fake-ass brother-man
Who smiled and clowned and claimed to be down,
Only to stab me in the back
When shit hit the fan –
don't you know blud, what it means to be fam?

I would rather spend my time, not waste it,
Manifesting the heart's true desire – I can taste it:
To free the mind and be at peace – can you dig it?
Cuz I can't take this shit no mo!

My Brother's Best Friend

Patricia Foster McKenley

My brother Andrew isn't going to school today.
Phillip has gone.

The night before, my brother
and some friends
sat on wooden chairs
around Phillip's bed
a lone island
in the middle of the living room,
and talked about playing cricket;
sniffing or rubbing eyes with sleeves
trying to sound upbeat. One person's laughter missing.
I sat on a small, beige, leather pouffe
near the telly, which was nonsense in the background
and my mum got up rushing out.
It was the first time I had seen her cry
in front of my brother and me.
Phillip's bald head
was the only light thing in the dimly lit room.
His eyelids were heavy, eyes rolling around underneath them.
I saw my brother's eyes dart everywhere around the room
stopping finally at Phillip's feet
shrunken and small under a purple and blue
crocheted bedcover.
My brother's best friend looked eleven
like me
instead of seventeen,
his muscles folded and tucked away,

prepared for a long rest.

Sons of the Chieftain

P. L. J. McIntosh

Their fam'ly folklore spoke of six.
Highland brothers. Five of whom left the loam
for this island; yet to be spiced *but ev'ryting nice*
volcanic made lush land. Now, many planter-sow-reap
seasons on, front room drenched in June indigo dusk,
we talk and mind walk *deh 'pon de lan's*:
we, the cinnamon and nutmeg hued.
The autumnal sunsets of russet.
The freckled burnish of ripe golden apple.
The duppy cream of sugar apple's flesh, sweet to the taste.
The eggplant-black of its tongue-polished seed.
A gathering, spilling into garden
like excess kinfolk cargo, sea-jettisoned.
A slow turning cane-press of heat,
oppressive as fettered passage supine,
extracts night's oxygen,
trailing molasses of breathlessness.
Its threat of rain overseeing,
cumulus bullwhip in hand:
and I wondered highland fives.
And kaleidoscope of kin
– their chocolate rainbow shimmering –
and them who *took* the name,
Emancipation offered,
of new no-longer owners.
The need to ask redundant:
like Master, to be satiated,
dusk found in negresse
quarters.

Home Again

Peter Kahn

In the red phone box across the street
from the Royal National Hotel (which
I just walked by yesterday – thirty years later)
I plink coins into a hungry mouth while tears
bump and grind in my eyes as I tell Dad,
I can't do this. I want to come home.
He's in Ohio and I'm three days into
a semester abroad in London that I'm
begging to make four days abroad and back
to Boston where my junior year of college parades
forward without me. My pocket was stuffed with
pounds but I reach in and only three still reside there.
Dad says, *Give it another week and we can
figure it out then.* I'm coinless and only get
out the *O* in *OK* before Dad is just a rude tone.
A week stammers by and then thirteen years
later I live here for two years. Then every
summer. Then again for a year six years ago
so that London is where Mom says, *Enjoy
your time back home.*

If We Were Real

Peter Raynard

Jo's mum Helen is a slag,
doesn't stop her having a go
at Jo getting pregnant by a black man
and staying in a hole
with that pansified little creep though.

Colin's mum is no better,
she's just after his dead dad's
insurance money, but Colin's
a little toerag running for his life,

who'll let the whole fucking lot
of them down. Arthur's a proper
hard bastard, working his seed
into as many women as he can.

And guess what, Victor's only gone
and got his missus up the ready rough,
so has to live with the mother-in-law,
and she's had a leading role

in working men's jokes for years.
Tommy's off up the match, an away game
kick-the-shit out of any proper casual
who'll have it. Ray beats up his missus
when he gets home, stamps on her throat

like some rat he found in the bog. Lol's dad
commits the horrors with her sister
and her mate any place he can, then tries
it on with her until Combo ends the cunt.

Young Timmy knows how to enjoy himself,
he cleans double-breasted windows,
or checks under the sink for some
scantily clad plumbing, before delivering

a whipped cream double entendre
to bored housewives. Rita likes a bit
of that an' all, off shagging Bob,
with her mate Sue, but her namesake

tries her hand at books instead of dotting
her luck on the bingo of a Saturday night.
Shirley's fucked off to Greece, can't stand
talking to the wall no more, cooking

egg 'n' chips for her husband,
who believes that's a woman's place.
Billy's dad knows what a man should be,
and it's not a fucking dancer.

Rent's smacked off his boat, so goes swimming
for a pearl in the filth of the bog,
whilst Dushane's a boy at the top
of his game, on the estates round his way.

Like Frank's kids, who surround him
like a wreath, this all may be true.
And Big Chris is right when he says,
It's been emotional.
But is that really all we are?
Do we not go by any other names?

The oracle bones of St Rish

Rishi Dastidar

I woke up this morning and I wasn't a saint,
again, so how else am I to mediate between
the human and the divine except rough marks?

One by one I pick up my four treasures of
the study until I am ready to leach the future
from the marrow of these oracle bones,

become a vertical brush for the King's Roman,
pickliftstrike my way into making meaningful
signs that mirror my hand, the true aperture

of my soul: stop looking at my eyes! The disquiet
is: I thought I was writing the folding book of me.
Turns out it was actually only a furious telegram.

Dinah's Brother

Roger Robinson

My tears have flowed in floods,
I am you brother and I have
prayed to this god above,
to test me instead of you.
It's still rape though he calls it love?
Bury me in a muddy grave
of shame before I let him hug
you as wife, I'll drain his life of blood.

Tattooing the Land

Rosanna Raymond

A large man has been felled
backed into a corner, revealing his tusks

They are engorged, his gaze enraged
he is flailing, falling on his haunches

mauling the walls
looking a bit dis'Hori'entated

Was it a woman who did this? No
Was it the gods? Maybe

I'm trying to figure out what they just said to me
The past blasted through my head so fast . . . it scrambled

leaving me a code to re-order
I see his shadow has gone out dancing

leaving him home alone with just his heart to engage with
every now and again it tremors

glowing with a fiery red underflow
burning everything that comes across it

tattooing the land

Don't worry say the gods, just take him to the open sea
Don't worry said the women, just give him to me

Another Woman's Scent

Sarah Reilly

Watching a film one Sunday afternoon
I glimpsed my first love, beyond the screen,
standing naked in an empty room.
I followed each frame until I saw him again,

just as he had been, his limbs long,
a strength he didn't yet know he had;
his copper hair made a halo around
his head and a crown around his tender sex.

I had almost forgotten his beauty, but remembered
he'd brought another woman's scent to our bed;
he wanted to bewitch me with jealousy.

And as I tasted the woman in his mouth, licked
her salt from his skin, felt her move in me as he
moved in me – I was bewitched, and wanted only her.

Vocabulary lessons

Soul Patel

Your swimming trunks have been pulled down and a word said you don't recognise. You turn around to see a cropped-haired blond boy your age looking at you. You're both in the water at the local leisure centre for a swimming class. The other children are nearby but not within earshot. You pull your trunks up. He spits this word at you again and swims off. You are as confused as you are hurt. You feel that something has changed.

Route

Sundra Lawrence

The news charcoals my fingers.
Syria is closed, I tell my daughter,
of course, she wants to know why:
The country is hurting itself –
people want to find safety.

She sketches a map on paper
from her toy globe
then colours in the countries,
she draws a route from Damascus to London:
It's so they can find us.

If they wear good shoes
can the Syrians walk through Turkey
and catch a boat to Greece?
I say it's a good plan
but crossing the water is costly.

Are there beds? Will their mummies tuck them in?
Families hold each other for the journey, I say,
I pull the covers up to her chin.
Her breath is all that remains of the day;
guiding the cheap rafts through rough seas.

Transcending the Bough

(After Brittney Leeanne Williams)

Tara Betts

To be above, to float, to rise, to crumble
within the dusk – rich, spectral
butterflies dipped in umber and kink,

pink as your palms and soles tickling
autumn leaves with tenderness
wavering like the opening of mouths.

Arc and flutter, you dance in the womb
of the sky among arteries and capillaries
reaching out as heavy branches. Understand

how roots twin that blood dance underground,
spread wider, deeper. All of you, all of us,
swimming, folding, lofty kicks in the air.

Someone will attempt to remind you,
even in this – a honeyed, cloudless
expanse – that people hid and died
in such cradles. You recall and still
levitate alive with unbound grace.

Soldier Ants

Tolu Agbelusi

I was eight when ants invaded
my bed. Burrowed a hole
through my window net, marched
in until my white sheets blackened
with oversized heads. Tiny bodies
exploring new routes under
my pyjamas, inside my armpits, thighs,
twirling an amulet from wrist to elbow.
Thousands of them matted together
in a black cloud, stapling into my skin.
A gradual constant burning. My face
was spared until howling invited
further invasion. I started to wonder
what it would take not to feel.

Ẹgbà mi! Báwo ni ìjàlọ Ṣe dé orí bed ẹ?
Mum scraped the clothes off, dunked
my body in a tub of cold water, soothed
my skin with calamine lotion.

I'm thirty-six now. Haven't forgotten. Ants
still follow – the lover who forgot
to remove his wedding band, the boss
who said bye with a letter on my desk,
the job centre queue every Tuesday
forcing the blinds to stay shut.

The ants multiply.

SiStar

Ugochi Nwaogwugwu

African
women hold up half the sky with
one hand on their hip

Ike Poem Form

Created by Ugochi Nwaogwugwu

In honour of #NationalPoetryMonth and in celebration of
#BlackLivesMatter, I have created a poetry form called *Ike* (pronounced
ē'kā). The *Ike* poem was born on April 24, 2015. *Ike* is an Igbo word that
means 'power'. An *Ike* resembles a haiku, but there is one major difference:
it is a Pan-African poem of sixteen syllables. The first line is three syllables,
one syllable for every letter in the word *red*; the second line is eight syllables
for *black and*, and the third line is five syllables, for *green*. An *Ike* should
invoke images inspired by Black life, freedom, redemption and power. If you
choose to write an *Ike* poem, use the hashtag #ikepoem and let's recreate the
impressions and images of Blackness for the betterment of Black life and the
global Black experience.

Midnight in the Foreign Food Aisle

Warsan Shire

Dear Uncle, is everything you love foreign
or are you foreign to everything you love?
We're all animals and the body wants what
it wants, trust me, I know. The blonde said
Come in, love, take off your coat, what do
you want to drink?

Love is not haram but after years of fucking
women who are unable to pronounce your name,
you find yourself totally alone, in the foreign
food aisle, beside the turmeric and saffron,
remembering your mother's warm, dark hands,
prostrating in front of the halal meat, praying in a
language you haven't used in years.

7up

Yomi Şode

My father rewards my good behaviour
though I have no idea what I've done.
He sits me down on our sofa, its ripped
edges pierce my skin. My shuffling is

mistaken for nerves, his Duchenne smile
a comedic tragedy of sorts, more Melpomene
than Thalia. There is little sparkle in his eyes
now, yet his shoulder eclipses the light bulb

as he stands and walks assured to the kitchen
bringing back a 7up bottle dripping in cold sweat.
He hooks his canine underneath the cap and pulls
downwards, I watch his silhouette in awe.

I hear the sound the bottle makes when placed
on the table. My father rewards my good behaviour
with 7up. He pours it in a glass only used for visitors –
for a moment, I see the dissipating foam as a dream,

he continues to gently pour then asks
Do any men enter the house when Daddy is at work?
a magician that knows when 7up reaches the rim
without overspill, without looking

I shake my head side to side, holding a stare he soon
breaks – *Am I in trouble now, Daddy?* He knuckles the
filled glass towards me, then sits back, listens to each
gulp. I thank him knowing I don't know the good I done.

Shakespeare Honours My Grandmother

Zakia Carpenter-Hall

On the day Grandma Ruth will be buried,
actors as pallbearers carry the likeness
of a body wrapped in white cloth,
held together with twine. The priest,

like those in Coptic churches, holds
a gold censer wafting frankincense,
known for its sweetness. The actress's
likeness is placed into a gravesite onstage

which happens to be under the thrones
of kings and moves on an axis. My grandmother's
funeral, four thousand miles away, has begun,
my only regret is that I am late to admission.

The theatre is so dark the usher can't see
where I am supposed to sit. She doesn't know
I am the granddaughter of the deceased,
but places me closer to the burial site,

nearer to those who grieve. I can touch
the procession, hum words to the funeral song.
I know this is not how Grandma Ruth's funeral
will go, her body carried from the highest point

to the lowest. There may be some African prints
but few bright colors, and no priest. I can see
the play, but also my grandmother's ancestral home –
how they welcome her today with ritual and song.

No

Zubaria Lone

No doesn't have to mean No
No means different things at different times
No stops us in our tracks
Dead

No means I know better
No means I control things and you don't
No means if you do what I say, we get on, if you don't, we won't
No means someone said No to me so I'm saying No to you

No stands for status quo
No means don't do anything
Don't change anything
And no one gets to point

But ...
No is tactical and No can change its mind
No is a starting point, No is a time to explore
No is a wall, No is an invitation to break through

No can be playful and No can be fun
But only when both know what No really means

Can No ever not be No?
Like the smiley lady who says No ...
When in doubt No means No, no matter what

So remember...
Don't get bothered
Don't get fussed
Because No
just means No

Eighteen steps to starting your own poetry collective

Malika Booker

The following is – roughly – what we did when we created Malika's Poetry Kitchen. I hope this how-to guide enables you to start your own poetry collective wherever you are in the world.

1. Think about what isn't there

It all began because Roger and I wanted to give back. We recognised that there was a void – no supportive community for writers of colour to be apprentices, to hone their skill, develop their craft in both writing and performance, reading, and giving and receiving feedback. We also wanted to pass forward the tools that our mentor Kwame Dawes had empowered us with. To encourage social engagement and professional support. To build up all of our poetics and enable each of us to find our voice. To encourage writers to find their own truth.

2. Draft a mission statement

So that the writers in the collective know what the aims of the collective are. Our mission statement was:

- To write, read, and listen to each other's work
- To willingly critique and accept critique, initiate artistic discussions, and support each other
- To aim for excellence

- To bring back to the group any knowledge discovered through personal research or from attending other workshops
- To meet regularly and consistently

3. Find a template to use as a model
We used June Jordan's *Poetry for the People: A Revolutionary Blueprint*. Maybe you will use these steps?

4. Find a venue, and set a regular time and day to meet
Roger and I decided to host the workshops in my house, as that seemed the easiest thing. In hindsight this really worked to encourage trust amongst the collective, and build a sense of family, community and generosity. Although you don't have to throw open your own doors, meeting, and meeting often, is key.

5. Always be on the lookout for members
Members are always looking for people who would benefit from our community – and who our community would benefit from. Members of Kitchen have been found at other workshops and performances, or through conversations with other poets. And we try to invite people face-to-face, rather than via email. It might also be worth running a 'get to know you' session for prospective new members, to see if the collective is right for them.
Don't be surprised if only one or two people come at first. The first Kitchen session consisted of Roger, me and one other poet. But the next week we had more members. The week after, more again . . .

6. Invite established poets as guest lecturers
We have had guests come and teach the collective since its birth. We can boast writers like Kei Miller, Olive Senior, Kim Moore and countless other poets. This enables us to be influenced and open to a variety of contemporary poetic practices, and is a vital resource for us.

7. Plan your session(s)
We planned all of our workshops, which usually followed this structure: first, writing exercises, using templates from published writers as examples, followed by sharing and critique. We initially used June Jordan's 'Guidelines for

Critiquing a Poem' as the template for giving feedback. Every session we read poems, interrogated them – and then wrote.

8. Be community-minded in your individual reading and writing practices

Roger and I are active readers, and are always bringing to Kitchen new poets we have discovered, or recommending a book about poetics. Visiting international poets stayed in our homes, so we developed a sense of community in both work and friendship. When we both applied and were accepted into The Complete Works (a development programme for Black and Asian poets in the UK), we did so in part to show our devotion to getting better at our craft, and to inspire our fellow writers in the collective.

9. Set up a safe space for writing

Because we started in my home people were relaxed in that space. We trained poets in the art of feedback, encouraging honest and truthful critique centered around the work, not the person. This enabled writers to feel safe enough to write about things they found difficult or were taboo. It was always our responsibility to enable each other's work to be the best that it could be.

10. Set milestones to bind the group

One of the ways we did this was through organising performances. It encouraged healthy competition as well as support – in creating work, rehearsing, choosing individual sets, yet making sure there was an overall narrative flow to the evening. We rehearsed, gave each other feedback, met for mic checks and run-throughs before going on stage. The pep talks and affirmations backstage before the performances were often the best part of the experience.

11. Do things together outside of poetry

Kitchen didn't just stop at my kitchen. We attended events together, had plenty of dinners together – we were at Wagamama *a lot*.

12. Members of the collective should always support and promote the collective

Kitchen is a space where people are encouraged to step up. Put poets up when they visit. Promote and attend other members' poetry events, and buy their books, always acknowledging the collective out in the world, to build awareness, audiences and readers. When Peter Kahn started Malika's Poetry Kitchen in the USA and asked us to go to Chicago to show support and lead a workshop over there, we went. One of the reasons that Malika's Poetry Kitchen has had so much exposure is due to the poets in it – both current members and alumni – always blowing its horn.

13. Support members to run their own sessions
It is vital to train and support members in how to lead sessions – it ensures that the writers develop their own skills, and that there is no sense of a hierarchy, that everyone has a voice. It means that people learn how to teach. Roger and I didn't hold ourselves aloof: I would be a student in Roger's workshops and vice versa. It also means that the collective is exposed to a variety of knowledge and insight, and it encourages members to bring new poems or poetics that they have discovered back to other members. It has also meant that someone has always stepped up to manage Kitchen and secure its existence: ownership is with the collective.

14. You don't need funding from outside
We have never applied for funding, and have always been a grassroots, community-led organisation.

15. Get members to pay a sub
Kitchen has three terms a year; members pay a fee of £20 per term. These 'subs' are invested right back into the collective, and are used to pay for the Friday night space, as well as a small fee to any guest poets we invite to teach.

16. Make sure your reading is diverse
One of our main objectives from the outset was to broaden our reading and influences, so it was reflective of diverse voices and poetics, national and international. We began with the multiple reading lists in June Jordan's book *Poetry for the People – A Revolutionary Blueprint*. We then moved on to buying and borrowing anthologies from the Poetry Library. Some influential anthologies included: *The United States of Poetry* (film and book) by Bob Holman, *In The Tradition: An Anthology of Young Black Writers* by Kevin Powell, *Aloud: Voices from the Nuyorican Poets Cafe*, *The Best American Poetry* (published every year), and *The Penguin Book of Caribbean Verse in English* ed by Paula Burnett. We also read and watched poetry solo theatre shows by writers like: Sarah Jones, Danny Hoch, Dael Orlandersmith, John Leguizamo. Some of our favourite poets were:

Sharon Olds, Naomi Shihab Nye, Li-Young Lee, Bob Hicok and Kwame Dawes. We were given permission by American poets as we saw ourselves reflected in the poets, and their poetics and poetry.

17. Document, document, document

Record everything. We did not – but in this time of mobile phones and other technology conducive to capturing memories and moments, you can. I urge you to learn from our oversight. Your archives will thank you.

18. Don't forget the snacks

Writing should be done over snacks and beverages of some sort. We currently meet in the offices of the Poetry School in London, so we have access to the kettle. But members are also encouraged to bring snacks – chocolate biscuits, sweets and crisps (unhealthy examples I know, but sadly accurate) might be some of the offerings passed around the table as we write. Remember: *a family that eats together, stays together.*

Contributors

Allison Lindner was born and raised in the English-speaking South American country of Guyana. She did a stint in Canada, and the UK has been her home for the past fifteen years. She is currently finishing a doctorate on sustainable development and the waste-management economy in South Africa at Kent Law School, thanks to funding from the Economic and Social Research Council. She is a practitioner of several forms of Afro-Brazilian dance and can speak with you in French and Portuguese. She was a member of Malika's Poetry Kitchen from 2009–2011. You can find her tweeting @allowrites

Anna Doležal's writing uncovers her response, as an immigrant, to cultural expectations in Britain. She considers her life and generations of her mother's family in India, the politics of coloniality and the way everyday life is still affected by those power relations. WW2 forced her father to leave Czechoslovakia; he spent the rest of his life stateless. How she feels and how she appears, often at odds, is an interface that will always be with her. Collective experience and insight are shared by connecting with others, and Malika's Poetry Kitchen offers her, as a poet, a global view of fightback.

Anne Enith Cooper has had poetry published in the Loose Muse Anthologies and *Proletarian Poetry*. She is the author of the pamphlet *Touched* and the antiwar poem-essay *21st-Century Guernica*, described as 'Powerful and deeply moving' by the late Tony Benn MP. She is an activist, and the writer-in-residence at Cressingham Gardens, an estate facing demolition. In 2017, her art and activism merged when she published *306: Living Under the Shadow of Regeneration*. She has performed poetry widely in the UK; at the Bowery Poetry NYC and promoted spoken-word events.

Aoife Mannix was born in Sweden of Irish parents. She grew up in Dublin, Ottawa and New York before moving to the UK. She has published four collections of poetry and a novel. She has previously been poet in residence for the Royal Shakespeare Company, the Portsmouth Museum and BBC Radio 4's *Saturday Live* amongst others. She has performed her poetry throughout the UK and internationally with the British Council. She has a PhD in creative writing from Goldsmiths, University of London. See aoifemannix.co.uk for more information.

Arji Manuelpillai is a poet, performer and creative facilitator based in London. For over fifteen years Arji has worked with community arts projects nationally and internationally. He is co-founder of children's theatre company A Line Art and is an advocate for arts as a tool for change. Recently, his poetry has been published by magazines including *Prole, The Cannon's Mouth, Strix, The Rialto* and *The Lighthouse Journal*. He has also been shortlisted for the Burning Eye BAME Poetry Competition 2018, the Robert Graves Prize 2018 and the Live Canon prize 2017. Arji is a member of Wayne Holloway-Smith's poetry group, Malika's Poetry Kitchen and London Stanza.

Referred to as 'the film-poet', **Be Manzini** has found ways to uniquely combine her passion for poetry, film and wellbeing. She is the first ever writer-in-residence for Sundance, poet-on-tour with numerous films, poet on the Mark Kermode MK3D live show and writing facilitator for Virgin Sport. Known for her ability to create universal and nurturing spaces, she was formerly the coordinator for Malika's Poetry Kitchen and the international exchange programme for the London Teenage Poetry Slam. A writer who has been resident at the Southbank Centre, and as a speaker and regular panelist at events, Manzini is also the Director of Caramel Film Club, spot-lighting Black talent and supporting diversity in film.

Bernadette Reed is a singer-songwriter who completed the Goldsmiths MA in Creative and Life Writing in 2012. She attended Malika's Poetry Kitchen in the months following for the experience of lively ongoing writing support. She is preparing a collection of poems about growing up in a small village in South Wales, from where she moved to London in the late seventies. An acupuncturist at the New Cross Natural Therapy Centre, she is a member of Southwark Stanza and Meantime Poets and hosts a monthly poetry and music open-mic with guests, which alternates between Greenwich and Deptford, called Talking Rhythm.

Cath Drake, an Australian who lives in London, has been published in anthologies and literary magazines in UK, Australia and US, and performed widely. She has been shortlisted for the Venture Poetry Award and the Manchester Poetry Prize, and was second in the 2017 Resurgence Poetry Prize for eco poetry. *Sleeping with Rivers* won the 2013 Mslexia Women's Poetry Pamphlet Competition and was the Poetry Book Society summer selection 2014. *The Shaking City* was published by Seren Books in 2020, with a poem highly commended in the Forward Prizes for Poetry. Her work includes environmental writing, award-winning journalism and teaching mindfulness. cathdrake.com

Charlotte Ansell recently returned to MPK after a ten-year hiatus during which she lived in Yorkshire. Her third poetry collection, *Deluge*, was published by flipped eye in November 2019 and was a PBS Winter Recommendation. She performs her poems regularly and her work has appeared in *Poetry Review*, *Mslexia, Now Then, Butcher's Dog, Prole, Algebra of Owls* and various anthologies. Charlotte won the Red Shed Open Poetry Competition, was one of six finalists in the BBC Write Science competition in 2015, won the Watermarks poetry competition and was commended in the YorkMix competition in 2016.

Christina Fonthes is a Congolese–British writer. Her mantra 'telling stories through any means possible' allows her to bring untold stories to life through her poetry and performances. Her work, laden with themes of womanhood, religion, and sexuality, has taken her all over the UK to perform. Her writing has been widely published in journals and anthologies worldwide. Christina is founder of REWRITE, a creative writing organisation for Black women and women of colour writers around the globe. Christina currently lives in London.

Cyril Husbands is a poet, storyteller, songwriter and performance artist, who makes an artistically compromised living as a management consultant. Cyril's abiding themes are relationships of every kind – familial, communal, social and political. His work is informed by his progressive Pan-Africanist politics and an abiding interest in human rights and justice. He works hard on making his output accessible, in the hope that audiences are engaged and inspired by what he has to say – particularly if they are prompted to create their own art.

Daniel Kramb is a writer and poet. He is the author of three novels: the story of a London rebellion, *Central* (2015); *From Here* (2012), about climate change; and the Hackney-set *Dark Times* (2010); and a booklet of poetry: *Timid Takes* (2013). *Look at Us* is a stage collaboration with the writer and poet JJ Bola. Daniel runs the Lonely Coot small press, and is collaborating with Jean Casey on Sin Scéal Eile, a listening project that turns life stories into poetry. Originally from Germany, Daniel lived in London for sixteen years, and is now based in Westcliff-on-Sea.

Dean Atta was named as one of the most influential LGBT people in the UK by the *Independent on Sunday*. He was shortlisted for the Polari First Book Prize for his debut poetry collection, *I Am Nobody's Nigger*. His poems have been anthologised by Bad Betty Press, Emma Press and Platypus Press, and appear in journals such as *Modern Poetry in Translation, The Scores* and the *Stockholm Review of Literature*. He is a tutor for Arvon and the Poetry School, a member of Keats House Poets Forum and Malika's Poetry Kitchen. His novel, *The Black Flamingo*, was published in 2019.

Dele Meiji Fatunla is a British-Nigerian writer. His non-fiction writing has appeared in a variety of publications including *Chimurenga*, the *Guardian*, *New Black Magazine, Modern African Generation, New African Woman* and the *New African*. His stories and poetry have been published in *Velocity: The Best of Apples & Snakes*, as well as *Saraba, Kwani?, Monochrome Lagos, Jalada Africa* and *Open Road Review*.

Denise Saul is a writer and poet. Her *White Narcissi* (flipped eye) was a Poetry Book Society Pamphlet Choice and *House of Blue* (Rack Press) was PBS Pamphlet Recommendation. She is a Geoffrey Dearmer Prize-winner. Denise is the founder of Silent Room: A Journey of Language, a collaborative video poem project, funded by Arts Council England.

Dorothea Smartt FRSL has two full poetry collections (Peepal Tree Press). Her chapbook *Reader, I Married Him & Other Queer Goings-On*, 'about Black diasporic love', is 'subversive, radical, and surprisingly panoramic'. Her collection *Ship Shape* is an A-Level English Literature text. For her contribution to British cultural life, she was nominated for a Barbados Golden Jubilee Award. In 2019 she was inaugurated a Fellow of the Royal Society of Literature. She is currently a Doctoral candidate at the University of the West Indies Cave Hill developing a new work: re-visioning same-sex relationships, and traditional spiritual practices, among 'West Indians' during the construction of the Panama Canal.

Elena Lagoudi is born in Greece. At twenty-one she runs away to London to explore the meta-punk scene and familiarise herself with tea. Six hundred parties and six ghastly jobs later, she finds herself at Tate Britain and then the National Gallery, working with the most inspiring teams of curators and educators in projects that increase museum access for diverse audiences. Clueless and hopeful, she returns to Greece in 2010 in order to experience Armageddon at its epicentre. Her writing experience ranges from museum labels and scripts to stodgy reports and poetry in English and Greek.

Esther Poyer writes about an imagined past from a rich Guyanese legacy, alongside the imagery and vernacular of her life as born and raised in 1980s London. These and other contrasting aspects resonate in her storytelling, where she draws on emotional responses to the tension between family relationships in unfamiliar environments. She writes to tell the stories of displacement and diaspora otherwise hidden from mainstream view, and to inspire people to listen and relate to one another. She has performed poetry and live literature in the UK and as far flung as Nairobi, Kenya.

Fikayo Balogun is a writer and spoken-word artist based in London. She has a Masters degree in Creative and Professional Writing from Roehampton University. She has performed in and won many spoken-word slams across Europe. Her works have also appeared in several magazines and anthologies. She has been a member of Malika's Poetry Kitchen for a number of years, writing alongside renowned writers. Fikayo grew up in Nigeria and moved to London alone as an adult; this can sometimes reflect in the use of language in her work. She is currently working on her first collection.

Touted in the *Independent* as 'a name to watch', **Gemma Weekes** is the critically acclaimed author of *Love Me* (Chatto & Windus), as well as a multidisciplinary artist, singer, musicmaker and poet who has performed nationally and internationally. Her work has appeared in several anthologies and literary journals including *IC3: The Penguin Book of New Black Writing in Britain* (Penguin), *Kin*

(Serpent's Tail), *Mechanic's Institute Review 14*, and most recently in *Filigree* (Peepal Tree Press), and she was recently shortlisted for the Bridport Prize for flash fiction. She has written for theatre, TV and radio and has scored various dance projects and short films.

Hannah Gordon is queer poet, writer and a Ciotóg. She is the co-organiser and host of Spoken Word London, a bi-monthly open mic night, is the founder of Words Down writing group, and is part of the inaugural mid-career poets' programme at the Roundhouse. She has performed at venues all over London and at festivals, she has won slams and her poetry has been published in various anthologies, including the 2019 *Anti-Hate Anthology*.

Harry Man won the UNESCO Bridges of Struga Award. His pamphlet *Lift* was shortlisted for a Best New Pamphlet Sabotage Award and his second, *Finders Keepers*, illustrated by the artist Sophie Gainsley, was shortlisted for the Ted Hughes Award for New Work in Poetry. His latest book is *Thereafter / Deretter* and is co-written with the poet Endre Ruset (Hercules / Flamme Forlag). You can find more of his work at manmadebooks.co.uk

Heather Taylor is a writer and director. She is an alumna of the 2018/19 Bell Media Prime Time TV Program (in association with ABC Signature Studios), and 2019 Corus Writer's Apprentice Program. She has developed shorts, web series and features – both narrative and documentary – and graduated with a Masters in screenwriting from City University, London. As a poet, she has three published collections: *Sick Day Afternoons, Horizon and Back*, and *She Never Talks of Strangers*. She's also been featured in numerous collections, and performed her work across Europe, Asia, and North America. See more at heancerataylor.com

Born in Nigeria, **Inua Ellams** is a cross-art form practitioner, a poet, playwright and performer, graphic artist and designer, and the founder of the Midnight Run – an international, arts-filled, night-time, playful, urban, walking experience. He is a The Complete Works poet alumnus and a designer at White Space Creative Agency. Across his work, identity, displacement and destiny are recurring themes in which he also tries to mix the old with the new: traditional African storytelling with contemporary poetry, pencil with pixel, texture with vector images. His poetry is published by flipped eye, Akashic, Nine Arches, Penned in the Margins, and several of his plays have been published by Oberon.

Jacob Sam-La Rose is a poet, educator, editor and creative technologist. He has performed and delivered programmes for poets across Europe, the US, Southern Africa and Southeast Asia. He has produced work on commission for the National Gallery, De Balie (Amsterdam), NitroBEAT and other institutions and cultural organisations. His collection *Breaking Silence* is studied at A-Level. His poetry has been translated into Portuguese, Latvian, French and Dutch.

Jamal 'Eklipse' Msebele is an award-winning poet, emcee and educator. His poetry pamphlet *Kaleidoscope* has garnered many accolades, including Libby Purves's response – 'a future Poet Laureate' – and is available on Amazon. His awards include the Betjeman Poetry Prize, the Foyle Young Poets Award and SLAMbassadors. He has also performed all over the UK and internationally. His most fond memories include opening for Saul Williams, performing alongside Chance the Rapper, and a private audience with De La Soul.

Janett Plummer's pamphlet *Lifemarks* is published by flipped eye, and reprinted in *The Mouthmark Book of Poetry*. She features in anthologies *Jubilation, RED, A Storm Between Fingers* and *Handmade Fire*. She is a member of Malika's Poetry Kitchen and Thea Poets. Her next poetry collection, *The architect of her undoing*, is due to be published. She is the founder of Inspired Word, a women's literature and mental health organisation, promoting poetry's therapeutic qualities. She was shortlisted for Spread the Word's London Short Story Prize, is a commended StorySLAM: Live finalist, and is the winner of four poetry slam titles. She won a Royal Literature Society Literature Matters award with Charlotte Ansell and together they curated and edited *Chosen?*, an anthology of writing about adoption, published by Aspire Creativity Press.

Jill Abram has always put pen to paper but started becoming a poet in 2007. She made her performance debut in 2008, joined Kitchen in 2009 and became its Director in 2010. She has won slams and competitions and been published in various journals and anthologies, including *Vanguard #3, Loose Muse, The Rialto, Magma*'s Deaf Issue, *And Other Poems* and *Ink, Sweat & Tears*. She produces and presents a variety of poetry events, including the Stablemates series of conversation and poetry. Jill grew up in Manchester, travelled the world and now lives in Brixton. jillabram.co.uk

Jocelyn Page is an American currently in London, where she lives with her partner and sons. She teaches English and Creative Writing at Goldsmiths, University of London and the University of London Worldwide. She published *smithereens* (tall-lighthouse) in 2010 and *You've Got to Wait Till the Man You Trust Says Go* (Argent) in 2016, as well as poems in the *Spectator, Poetry Review* and *Poetry Ireland Review*.

Joey Connolly grew up in Sheffield and studied at the University of Manchester. He founded and edited the poetry journal *Kaffeeklatsch* and was the manager of the Free Verse: Poetry Book Fair for several years. He is currently the head of Faber Academy. His poems have appeared in *Poetry Review*, the *Sunday Times*, *Poetry London*, *The Best British Poetry 2014* (Salt) and on BBC Radio 4. He received an Eric Gregory Award in 2012, and his first collection, *Long Pass*, was published by Carcanet in 2017.

Joolz Sparkes is a north London-based writer; her poetry appears in *Magma*, *South Bank Poetry* and *Shooter Literary* magazines, Loose Muse and Great Weather for MEDIA anthologies, and *Ink, Sweat & Tears* webzine. She was Poet-in-Residence at Leicester Square Tube station, has been shortlisted for the Bridport Poetry Prize, longlisted for Cinnamon Press and Live Canon pamphlet competitions, and has featured at Ledbury Poetry Festival. Her first poetry collection, *London Undercurrents*, a joint project with poet Hilaire, was published by Holland Park Press in 2019 and uncovers London's unsung hero-ines north and south of the river.

Kareem Parkins-Brown is a proud North-West Londoner, Barbican Young Poet alumnus and the 2019 Roundhouse Poetry Slam winner. His collaborators include the Barbican Centre and Tate Britain. You can find more at Twitter: @kalmtree and Instagram: @kalm.tree

Katie Griffiths grew up in Ottawa, Canada, in a family originally from Northern Ireland. She joined the Malika's Poetry Kitchen family in the autumn of 2014, and in 2016 was published in *Primers Volume One* by Nine Arches Press. In 2019 she won second prize in the National Poetry Competition, and her pamphlet *My*

Shrink is Pregnant was a winner in Live Canon's first pamphlet competition. Her first full-length collection, *The Attitudes*, was published in April 2021 by Nine Arches Press. Katie is singer-songwriter in the band A Woman in Goggles.

Karen McCarthy Woolf is a poet, broadcaster and editor of five literary anthologies. Her poems are translated into Spanish, Turkish, Italian, Dutch and Swedish. Her collection *An Aviary of Small Birds* was described as a 'pitch-perfect debut' (*Guardian*); her latest, *Seasonal Disturbances*, explores climate crisis, migration, the city and the sacred. Bridget Minamore says it 'feels like watching an avant-garde disaster movie: small slices of information swirling amongst the fast-moving scenes'. A The Complete Works alumna, Karen is a Fulbright Postdoctoral Scholar at UCLA where she is Writer-in-Residence for the Promise Institute for Human Rights.

Kayo Chingonyi is the author of two poetry pamphlets, and a fellow of the Complete Works programme for diversity and quality in British Poetry. In 2012, he was awarded a Geoffrey Dearmer Prize, and was Associate Poet at the Institute of Contemporary Arts (ICA) in 2015. His first full-length collection, *Kumukanda*, won the Dylan Thomas Prize and a Somerset Maugham Award and was shortlisted for the Costa Poetry Prize. It was also shortlisted for the Seamus Heaney Centre First Poetry Collection Prize, the Ted Hughes Award for New Work in Poetry, the Roehampton Poetry Prize and the Jhalak Prize. Kayo was a Burgess Fellow at the Centre for New Writing, University of Manchester before joining Durham University as Assistant Professor of Creative Writing. He is Poetry Editor at Bloomsbury and writer and presenter of the music and culture podcast *Decode* on Spotify. His latest collection of poems, *A Blood Condition* (Chatto & Windus, 2021), is a PBS Recommendation and his first work of nonfiction, *Prodigal*, is forthcoming from 4th Estate.

Khairani Barokka is an Indonesian writer, poet, and artist in London, whose work has been presented extensively, in sixteen countries. She was *Modern Poetry in Translation*'s inaugural Poet-in-Residence and a UNFPA Indonesian Young Leader Driving Social Change, and is now Research Fellow at UAL's Decolonising Arts Institute, and Associate Artist at the National Centre for Writing. Okka is creator of solo show 'Eve and Mary Are Having Coffee', and is most recently co-editor of *Stairs and Whispers: D/deaf and Disabled Poets Write Back* (Nine Arches Press), author-illustrator of *Indigenous Species* (Tilted

Axis; Vietnamese translation with AJAR), and author of poetry collection *Rope* (Nine Arches). khairanibarokka.com

Kostya Tsolakis is a London-based poet and journalist, born and raised in Athens, Greece. A Warwick Writing Programme graduate, his poems have been published in *Magma, perverse, Under the Radar* and *Wasafiri*, among others, while his translations have appeared in *Modern Poetry in Translation*. In 2019, he won the Oxford Brookes International Poetry Competition (ESL category). He founded and co-edits *harana poetry*, the online magazine for poets writing in English as a second or parallel language, and is poetry editor at *Ambit*. His debut poetry pamphlet, *Ephebos*, is out with **ignition**press. You can find him on Twitter: @kostyanaut

mae is an interdisciplinary artist working and experimenting with words, sound, movement and visual material. She has performed poems with the Oxford Stanza Group, the Back Room Poets, and Malika's Poetry Kitchen, and has poems published in magazines *The Dawntreader, Under the Radar* and *The Nail*. maeartist.com

Maisie Lawrence is an English–American poet and editor. For three years she orchestrated the Forward Prizes for Poetry, where she fell for contemporary poetry and met Malika Booker. She's been published in magazines including *The Rialto* and was shortlisted for the Strokestown Poetry Competition in 2018. She's been longlisted for the London Writers' Awards, Poetry School Primers and the Jerwood/Arvon Mentoring Programme. She is currently the recipient of Arts Council England funding to develop her first collection. She publishes fiction and is a co-founder of Pride in Publishing, a network for LGBTQ+ people who work with books. @maisiefrances

Malika Booker is a British poet of Guyanese and Grenadian parentage, and the founder of Malika's Poetry Kitchen. Her pamphlet *Breadfruit* (flipped eye, 2007) received a Poetry Society Recommendation, and her poetry collection *Pepper Seed* (Peepal Tree Press, 2013) was shortlisted for the OCM Bocas prize and the Seamus Heaney Centre 2014 First Collection Poetry Prize. She is published with the poets Sharon Olds and Warsan Shire in the third Penguin Modern Poets Series book, titled *Your Family, Your Body* (2017). Malika received her MA from Goldsmiths, University of London and has recently begun a PhD at the University of Newcastle. She was the Douglas Caster Cultural Fellow in Creative Writing at Leeds University, the first British poet to be a fellow at Cave Canem and the inaugural Poet-in-Residence at the Royal Shakespeare Company. Malika hosts and curates New Caribbean Voices, Peepal Tree Press's literary podcast, and is currently a poetry lecturer at Manchester Metropolitan University. 'The Little Miracles', originally published in *Magma*'s Loss issue, won the 2020 Forward Prize for Best Single Poem.

Whilst caring for her father, who was suffering from Alzheimer's, **Mary Renouf** and her father found themselves in a kind of shared liminal space, which surprised their world, changed their lives and charged their creativity. Since then, Mary, Joanna Procter, together with partners from Reveal Productions, were awarded a grant from the Solutions for an Ageing Society fund to make a film, *Care As You Are*, about the emotional impact of suddenly becoming a carer for a friend or relative living with dementia. The film is currently being developed (with support from Somerset Adult Social Care) as a training resource to support carers and all relevant associations to do with care.

Mehmet Izbudak was a London-based – now Norwich-based – playwright and poet, whose daytime jobs included being an Academic Teaching Developer at SOAS and a sessional lecturer at Birkbeck College, University of London. His stage scripts include an adaptation of Dostoevsky's novel *The Demons* and *Dr and Mrs Faustus*, a contemporary marketing tragicomedy. He joined Malika's Poetry Kitchen in 2014. He is also a member of the South Bank-based poetry collective, Tideway Poets. Mehmet is presently working on a translation of Polish poet Halina Poświatowska's works.

Melanie Mauthner is a translator of French literature. She joined Malika's Poetry Kitchen in 2010. Since then, she has been awarded a Hawthornden Fellowship and the French Voices Grand Prize 2013 for *Our Lady of the Nile*, her translation of Scholastique Mukasonga's novel. Her translations of Mukasonga's short fiction have appeared in the *New Yorker*, *The White Review* and the *New England Review*. Melanie's poems and stories have been published in magazines and anthologies. She lives in London.

Michelle Penn's debut pamphlet, *Self-portrait as a diviner, failing*, won the 2018 Paper Swans Poetry Pamphlet Prize. Her poems have appeared widely in journals, including *B O D Y, Finished Creatures, The Tangerine, Magma, Shearsman* and *The Pedestal*. She was shortlisted for the 2018 Aesthetica Creative Writing Prize and one of her poems inspired a jazz piece by composer Sarah Woolfenden. Michelle has read her work on Resonance FM and was interviewed on the BBC Radio 4 documentary, 'The Noisy Page'. She plans innovative literary events as part of the collective Corrupted Poetry. A dual UK/US national, she also writes fiction.

Naomi Woddis is a photographer, writer and radio-show host whose photography includes portraiture and still-life. The aim of her work is to be clear, compassionate and honest. She is also interested in opening new dialogues about mental health and chronic invisible illness, living with both herself. She hosts a radio show *The Two of Us* on Reel Rebels Radio, in which she talks to writers and artists about their work and how it relates to mental health and emotional wellbeing. Publishing credits include *Jupiter, Wasifari, Rising, Libertine, Split Screen, Double Bill* and *Stairs and Whispers* poetry anthologies.

Nick Makoha is the founder of The Obsidian Foundation. In 2017, Nick's debut collection, *Kingdom of Gravity,* was shortlisted for the Felix Dennis Prize for Best First Collection and was one of the *Guardian*'s best books of the year. Nick is a Cave Canem Graduate Fellow and the Complete Works alumnus. He won the 2015 Brunel International African Poetry Prize and the 2016 Toi Derricotte & Cornelius Eady Chapbook Prize for his pamphlet *Resurrection Man*. His poems have appeared in the *Cambridge Review,* the *New York Times, Poetry Review, The Rialto, Poetry London, TriQuarterly Review, Boston Review, Callaloo* and *Wasafiri.* He is a trustee for the Arvon Foundation and the Ministry of Stories, and a member of the Malika's Poetry Kitchen collective. nickmakoha.com

Nii Ayikwei Parkes is a Ghanaian writer and editor who has won acclaim as a children's author, poet, broadcaster and novelist. Winner of multiple international awards including Ghana's ACRAG award, his novel *Tail of the Blue Bird* won France's two major prizes for translated fiction – Le Prix Baudelaire and Le Prix Laure-Bataillon – in 2014. He was the founding director of the Aidoo Centre for Creative Writing in Accra and is the founder of flipped eye publishing, a leading small press. Nii Ayikwei serves on the boards of World Literature Today and the Caine Prize and is the current Producer of Literature and Talks at Brighton Festival.

Orishanti is a Nigerian and British griot. His time at Malika's Poetry Kitchen was invaluable to his development and he remains forever grateful for the good vibes and insightful critique. Read more at orishanti.wordpress.com

Patricia Foster McKenley is a Malika's Poetry Kitchen founder member and alumna. An award-winning poet and Inscribe-contracted writer, she was Sable Poet-in-Residence at Mboka Festival (Gambia) 2017. Born in Lewisham, her writing is inspired by Jamaican British heritage and champions women and survivors. A life coach to artists, Patricia facilitates workshops, including for the BBC, Every Woman Inspired (Jamaica), universities and schools. Patricia is published in anthologies and publications in the UK, Norway and the USA; she has performed in the Netherlands, Norway, the USA, Jamaica, Belgium and Gambia, and has toured the UK, Europe and the USA. In 2013, she released her first poetry film *LIPS*.

P. L. J. McIntosh is a writer of Afro-Caribbean heritage. He was an active member of Malika's Poetry Kitchen from 2006–9. His work has featured a series of poems that allowed him to explore his heritage and upbringing from a born and bred, Black British citizen's perspective. A former stockbroker, he is working towards becoming a full-time writer. He is currently completing his first chapbook.

A high school teacher based in Chicago, **Peter Kahn** runs the largest school-based Spoken Word Club in the world. He has twice been a commended poet in the Poetry Society's National Poetry Competition. He co-founded the London Teenage Poetry Slam and, as a Visiting Fellow at Goldsmiths, founded the Spoken Word Education Training Programme. Peter earned an MFA in Creative Writing from Fairfield University. Along with Patricia Smith and Ravi Shankar, Peter co-edited *The Golden Shovel Anthology: New Poems Honoring Gwendolyn Brooks*. His first collection, *Little Kings*, was published by Nine Arches Press in June 2020.

Peter Raynard is editor of *Proletarian Poetry: Poetry of Working Class Lives* (proletarianpoetry.com). He had two books of poetry published in 2018, his debut collection *Precarious* (Smokestack Books), and *The Combination: A Poetic Coupling of the Communist Manifesto* (Culture Matters).

Rishi Dastidar is a fellow of the Complete Works, a consulting editor at *The Rialto* magazine, a member of Malika's Poetry Kitchen, and chair of writer development organisation Spread the Word. A poem from his debut collection *Ticker-tape* was included in *The Forward Book of Poetry 2018*. A pamphlet, *the break of a wave*, was published by Offord Road Books in 2019, and he is editor of *The Craft: A Guide to Making Poetry Happen in the 21st Century* (Nine Arches Press). His second collection, *Saffron Jack*, is published in the UK by Nine Arches Press.

Roger Robinson is a writer who has performed worldwide and is an experienced workshop leader and lecturer on poetry. His one-man shows are *The Shadow Boxer*; *Letter from My Father's Brother*; and *Prohibition*. He was chosen by Decibel as one of fifty writers who have influenced the Black British writing canon. He is an alumnus of The Complete Works. He was shortlisted for the OCM Bocas Poetry Prize, the Oxford Brookes Poetry Competition, and was highly commended by the Forward Prize 2013. His *A Portable Paradise* won the T. S. Eliot Prize and the Royal Society of Literature's Ondaatje Prize in 2020. He has toured extensively with the British Council and is a co-founder of both Spoke-Lab and Malika's Poetry Kitchen.

Sistar S'pacific a.k.a. **Rosanna Raymond** is an innovator of the contemporary Pasifika art scene as a long-standing member of the art collective the Pacific Sisters, and founding member of the SaVAge K'lub. Raymond has achieved international renown for her performances, installations, body adornment, and spoken word. A published writer and poet, her works are held by museums and private collectors throughout the UK, USA, Canada, Australia and New Zealand.

Sarah Reilly is a maverick: her written work has been published in various poetry anthologies, and her visual art exhibited widely; her performances have drawn on a breadth of creative media. The subject matter is personal, social, and philosophical; she offers thoughtful perspectives on issues that are important to many of us: sexuality and gender, our responsibility as the dominant species, and what it means to be human. Contemporary ideas are embraced and filtered through a creative perspective, where imagination and philosophy merge, sometimes collide. Sarah Reilly lives in Brixton and is a psychotherapist.

Soul Patel is a London-based poet, and the themes of family and love are key to his poetry. His poems have been published in various literary journals including *Magma* and *The Rialto*, and he has also read his work at Keats House and at Cambridge University. Soul was a prize-winner in the Magma and Troubadour poetry competitions, runner-up in the Ambit Poetry Competition, was longlisted four years in a row in the National Poetry Competition, commended in the Magma Open Poetry Pamphlet Competition and shortlisted for the Complete Works Poetry Programme.

Sundra Lawrence is a poet and creative writing tutor. She has performed her work in venues ranging from Queen Elizabeth Hall, Southbank and Soho Theatre to Bristol Poetry Festival, as well as jazz cafés in Prague, and schools and venues in Chicago. Sundra's work has been broadcast on BBC2 and radio and is published in numerous anthologies including the *Los Angeles Review*. Her workshops and residencies include the Arvon Foundation; New Writing North; Apples & Snakes; the London Teenage Poetry Slam and the Royal Geographical Society amongst others. Sundra joined Malika's Poetry Kitchen in 2002.

Tara Betts is the author of *Break the Habit* and *Arc & Hue*. In addition to her work as a teaching artist and mentor for young poets, she has taught at several universities, including Rutgers University and University of Illinois at Chicago, and at Stateville Prison via Prison + Neighborhood Arts Project. Tara is Poetry Editor at *The Langston Hughes Review*. Dr. Betts is in the process of establishing the nonprofit organization The Whirlwind Learning Center on Chicago's South Side.

Tolu Agbelusi is a Nigerian–British poet, playwright, producer, educator and lawyer. Shortlisted for the 2018 White Review Poetry Prize, she's been published nationally and internationally, led guest lectures at universities and been commissioned widely. Her first poetry collection, *Locating Strongwoman*, was published by Jacaranda in 2020.

Ugochi Nwaogwugwu is a multidisciplinary creative who lives in Chicago and works in the world. A child of Nigeria, West Africa, her global sound and words pay homage to her homeland. Ugochi is an international singer, songwriter, poet, performer, educator and activist. Her personal, distinctive style expresses the vibrant spirit and atmosphere of the Igbo culture worldwide. Ugochi has written, performed and executive-produced three albums, *African Buttafly*, *ASE /Afro Soul Ensemble* and *Love Shot* on her independent label Spirit Speaks, Inc. Her poems have been featured in the anthologies *A Storm Between Fingers* (UK) and *The Golden Shovel Anthology* (USA). Ugochi is a member of the AACM and the Recording Academy.

Warsan Shire is a Somali British writer and poet. She was awarded the inaugural Brunel International African Poetry Prize, served as the first Young Poet Laureate of London, is the author of two chapbooks, *Teaching My Mother How to Give Birth* and *Her Blue Body*, is the youngest-ever member of the Royal Society of Literature, and is included in the Penguin Modern Poets series alongside Sharon Olds and Malika Booker. She provided the poetry for the Peabody Award-Winning visual album *Lemonade* and the film *Black Is King* in collaboration with Beyoncé Knowles-Carter, and wrote the short film *Brave Girl Rising*.

Yomi Ṣode is a Nigerian–British writer, performer, facilitator and The Complete Works alumnus. He has read poems at Lagos International Poetry Festival, Afrika Fest with Speaking Volumes in Finland, the New York Public Library with the British Council and at Edinburgh International Book Festival. His writing has been published in *The Rialto, Bare Lit Anthology, Ten: Poets of the New Generation* anthology, *Tales of Two Londons* anthology and the upcoming *Safe: On Black British Men Reclaiming Space*. In 2019 Yomi was awarded one of three Jerwood Compton Poetry Fellowships. *COAT*, Yomi's first one-man show, has toured nationally to sold-out audiences and he is currently working on his first poetry collection and second show.

Zakia Carpenter-Hall is a writer and facilitator from the US who currently lives in England. She holds an MFA in Creative Writing (Distinction) from Kingston University in London, and is a winner of *Poetry London*'s inaugural Mentoring Scheme. Her poems have appeared in visual poetry exhibitions and publications such as *Callaloo Journal, Magma* and *Wild Court*. She is the author of *Event Horizon* published by Sampson Low. Her poetry reviews and essays have been published by *Poetry London, Wild Court* and *Poetry Review*.

Zubaria Lone is a Malika's Poetry Kitchen alumna.

Acknowledgements

'The Last Compass Point' was first published in *Handmade Fire* (Mouthmark Press, 2006).

'My Brother's Best Friend' was published in the *Loose Muse* (2012).

'Miss Birdie's Letter//A Coupling' was first broadcast on BBC Radio 3's 'Between the Ears' in 2018.

'If We Were Real' was first published in *Precarious* (Smokestack Books, 2018).

'Midnight in the Foreign Food Aisle' was first published in *Her Blue Body* (flipped eye publishing, 2015).

For being so generous with their time, stories and memories, Daniel sends special thanks to: Jill Abram, Malika Booker, Patricia Foster McKenkley, Peter Kahn, Sundra Lawrence, Nick Makoha, Nii Ayikwei Parkes, Roger Robinson, Jacob Sam-La Rose, Denise Saul, and Nathalie Teitler.

Full copyright details

At the corner of New Market and East © Allison Lindner, 2021
Decline past tense: 'say' © Anna Doležal, 2021
This is a prayer © Anne Enith Cooper, 2021
Fire © Aoife Mannix, 2021
Tulips © Arji Manuelpillai, 2021
The Last Compass Point © Be Manzini, 2021
In varying dilutions © Bernadette Reed, 2021
Birthday © Cath Drake, 2021
Grimhilde's eclipse © Charlotte Ansell, 2021
Rebirth © Christina Fonthes, 2021
Return © Cyril Husbands, 2021
At the Edge of a Terrain © Daniel Kramb, 2021
Ode to My Cuticles © Dean Atta, 2021
Tube Pass © Dele Meiji Fatunla, 2021
Someone Walked into a Garden © Denise Saul, 2021
Elephantine © Dorothea Smartt, 2021
Divorce Petition to HM Court of the Family Division, Mordor, Middle-earth
    © Elena Lagoudi, 2021
The Carpenter © Esther Poyer, 2021
My Headstone Read 'Beloved Daughter' © Fikayo Balogun, 2021
(The Rhetoric Of.) © Gemma Weekes, 2021
Home © Hannah Gordon, 2021
Things to Consider Before Your First Spacewalk © Harry Man, 2021
On the Wall © Heather Taylor, 2021
Some Turn / To violence © Inua Ellams, 2021
For the Young Men Popping Wheelies on Southwark Street in Late Afternoon
    Traffic © Jacob Sam-La Rose, 2021
Kaleidoscope © Jamal 'Eklipse' Msebele, 2021
Alphabet © Janett Plummer, 2021
Twenty-two Months © Jill Abram, 2021

This unexpected longing for what I've always wished away © Jocelyn Page, 2021
The Claim © Joey Connolly, 2021
Five days and counting © Joolz Sparkes, 2021
Boomting © Kareem Parkins-Brown, 2021
Miss Birdie's Letter//A Coupling © Karen McCarthy Woolf, 2021
Cloister © Katie Griffiths, 2021
Chingola Road Cemetery © Kayo Chingonyi, 2021
mati lampu, jakarta © Khairani Barokka, 2021
London Fields © Kostya Tsolakis, 2021
black star © mae, 2021
Marianne © Maisie Lawrence, 2021
An Alternative History of Stones © Malika Booker, 2021
Who what are we? © Mary Renouf, 2021
Accidental memory © Mehmet Izbudak, 2021
The Demoiselle Crane © Melanie Mauthner, 2021
Truncated checklist for a Gothic novel © Michelle Penn, 2021
Hotel © Naomi Woddis, 2021
How a City Vanishes © Nick Makoha, 2021
Vogue © Nii Ayikwei Parkes, 2021
Ashes and Dust © Orishanti, 2021
My Brother's Best Friend © Patricia Foster McKenley, 2021
Sons of the Chieftain © P. L. J. McIntosh, 2021
Home Again © Peter Kahn, 2021
If We Were Real © Peter Raynard, 2021
The oracle bones of St Rish © Rishi Dastidar, 2021
Dinah's Brother © Roger Robinson, 2021
Tattooing the Land © Rosanna Raymond, 2021
Another Woman's Scent © Sarah Reilly, 2021
Vocabulary lessons © Soul Patel, 2021
Route © Sundra Lawrence, 2021
Transcending the Bough © Tara Betts, 2021
Soldier Ants © Tolu Agbelusi, 2021
SiStar © Ugochi Nwaogwugwu, 2021
Midnight in the Foreign Food Aisle © Warsan Shire, 2021
7up © Yomi Ṣode, 2021
Shakespeare Honours My Grandmother © Zakia Carpenter-Hall, 2021
No © Zubaria Lone, 2021